# ENTREPRENEURS WHO BUILT INDIA

**Praise for the Book**

'The first in the Entrepreneurs Who Built India series, this book will help readers understand why Gujarmal Modi was often called an audacious entrepreneur. Sonu Bhasin's book traces the industrialist's journey, from scratch to being one of the top industrialists of pre-liberalized India.'

—Harsh Mariwala, *chairman, Marico*

'The breadth of experience captured in Sonu Bhasin's *Gujarmal Modi: The Resolute Industrialist* reflects the gritty yet joyful journey of an entrepreneur towards success. The collective glory of independent India is actually a combination of many such individual efforts. The book will inspire future entrepreneurs.'

—Kuldip Singh Dhingra, *chairman, Berger Paints*

'This is the story of a true legend of Indian industry who can claim the title of the "father of manufacturing". Gujarmalji was a towering personality. He was instrumental in making Modinagar the capital of India's industrial map and it remains a testimony to an era when a giant of a man full of spirit and gumption walked the earth. A true hero!'

—Harsh Goenka, *chairman, RPG Enterprises*

'Sonu Bhasin has brilliantly narrated the life story of Gujarmal Modi, a unique personality who with great determination and perseverance built a business empire in India during very challenging times. He was amongst a handful of entrepreneurs who laid the foundation for the growth of Indian industry. Filled with lots of learnings and insights, this book is a must-read.'

—Muthu Murugappan, *head, strategy, EID Parry Ltd*

# ENTREPRENEURS WHO BUILT INDIA

# GUJARMAL MODI

## THE RESOLUTE INDUSTRIALIST

SONU BHASIN

HARPER
BUSINESS
*An Imprint of* HarperCollins *Publishers*

First published in India by Harper Business
An imprint of HarperCollins *Publishers* 2022
4th Floor, Tower A, Building No. 10, Phase II, DLF Cyber City,
Gurugram, Haryana – 122002
www.harpercollins.co.in

2 4 6 8 10 9 7 5 3 1



P-ISBN: 978-93-5489-474-9
E-ISBN: 978-93-5489-476-3



Cover design: HarperCollins *Publishers* India
Author photo: A Kumar

Typeset in 11.5/15.7 Warnock Pro at
Manipal Technologies Limited, Manipal

Printed and bound at
Thomson Press (India) Ltd

HarperCollinsIn

This book is produced from independently certified FSC® paper
to ensure responsible forest management.

*To the two men in my life – Juggi and Karan: You guys are my anchors in the choppy seas of life*

# *Contents*

# *Preface*

I find it an irony of fate that Gujarmal Modi—founder of India's seventh largest business empire in the 1960s—is today better known as the grandfather of Lalit Modi—the one of IPL fame. From being called a 'dirty Indian' by an Englishman in pre-Independence India to being banished from the princely state of Patiala; from setting up some of the finest factories in pre-Independence India to being coerced to follow the Indian government's diktat—Gujarmal Modi saw it all. But he was undaunted in his endeavour to set up some of the best and largest industries in India. Starting off with a single sugar mill in 1934, Gujarmal Modi, almost single-handedly, expanded his business to become one of the biggest industrialists in India by the 1960s. After his death in 1976, the business empire fell apart but even today, some of the industries set up by him and his inheritors survive and are worth over $2 billion collectively.

Gujarmal Modi and the Modi Group are not a lone example of thriving business empires set up in pre-Independence India that grew in stature and size in the following years and then lost their way as they were hit either by family feuds or liberalization or both. The Indian industrial and corporate sectors are scattered with people and businesses who lost their way after they saw their glory peak in the days that some consider to be the most challenging in the lives of Indian businessmen—the years between 1947 and 1991.

India became independent in 1947 and the new-found freedom brought forth aspirations and dreams for not just individuals, but also collective dreams of social, political and economic freedom. However, the first prime minister envisaged a developmental model that had the state playing a dominant role as an entrepreneur as well as the funder of private businesses. The dreams of the economic freedom that entrepreneurs had dreamt of in the new India quickly withered away as the British Raj was replaced by the Licence Raj.

Due to the restrictions placed by the Licence Raj, which many say was a complex and opaque system, being an entrepreneur in India was a big headache. Further, the entrepreneurial spirit was kept on a tight leash by the complex and authoritative system. Entrepreneurs were successful not so much because of what they did but because of who they knew. Such was the dependence on the benign hand of the government that businessmen, due to their association with politicians and bureaucrats, were also enveloped in the cloud of corruption in the minds of the general public.

However, people forget that there were many entrepreneurs, and indeed businesses, during those particularly challenging times that worked tirelessly to make the new India. Gujarmal

Modi was one of them. It certainly was not easy, but he persevered.

As an entrepreneur during the British rule, Gujarmal Modi faced problems around transport, logistics, communication and even skilled talent. The transport of most materials and supplies was on slow-moving carts or using the very few motor vehicles available. Getting in touch with mills and factories in remote locations was tough. Most machinery had to be imported and then it was a challenge to find workers to run the machines. There were no MBA institutes to churn out batches of management students who could run businesses; most entrepreneurs relied on family members to run the various businesses.

Some of these challenges persisted in independent India while some fresh ones were added. These new challenges primarily revolved around the new 'system' of doing business in independent India. True, Gujarmal Modi did learn how to 'manage' the system, but it required entrepreneurial skills to set up, manage and grow the businesses within the tight framework of the system. Manufacturing is never an easy business and the Licence Raj made achieving economies of scale even more difficult with the restrictions on the numbers that could be produced. It is to the credit of Gujarmal Modi that he not only went about his work diligently but also created products that became household names at that time. Unfortunately, most of those are present today either in a diluted form or are almost forgotten.

However, what cannot and should not be forgotten is Gujarmal Modi's contribution in being part of a group of entrepreneurs who worked to lay down the foundations of the Indian economy and industry. If it were not for him and other stalwarts who worked against the odds and set up businesses, provided employment to many people and kept the Indian economy growing, the India of today would not be where she is currently.

Thus, it is important to bring these entrepreneurs out of their obscurity and present them to the new generation as the entrepreneurs who made India.

This is the story of Gujarmal Modi, the founder of the Modi Group, which grew to be a large and diversified business empire by the late 1960s. It was a group with interests in sugar, steel, oil, vanaspati, tyres, nylon thread, yarn, lanterns, soaps and dehydrated food, among others. The story of Gujarmal Modi is not that of rags to riches; it is a story of a single man's determination to set up an industrial township of his own.

Gujarmal Modi came from a wealthy family—a family of businessmen who made their money by supplying goods to the British Army. Gujarmal was the eldest son of the family and could have taken the easy way out by managing his father's business. However, entrepreneurship and ambition burnt bright in young Gujarmal Modi, and he wanted to break out from under his father's shadow and establish businesses of his own.

Most entrepreneurs, when they start their entrepreneurial journey, have a vision of establishing a group of thriving businesses. Gujarmal Modi was different. When he started his independent entrepreneurial journey in 1933 with ₹300 in his pocket, his vision was to establish an industrial township. A thriving township with mills, factories, housing colonies for the workers, educational institutes, hospitals, shops and markets, temples and gardens.

He did set up his township and, in ten years' time, the town was named after him. Modinagar came into existence in 1945. And Gujarmal Modi's business empire continued to grow.

The following pages tell you the story of Gujarmal Modi, his life, his family and his entrepreneurship. As I spent time with Gujarmal Modi—vicariously, of course—reading about him, talking to people about him and listening to diverse people describing not only the man but also the times in which he operated, I understood the man a little better. He was not only an entrepreneur who set out to create an industrial township, he was also a deeply religious man. He was a caring employer, but he was also ruthless when it came to matters of business.

The man I got to know, as I wrote about him, was a man of many contradictions. He had strength of character but displayed vulnerabilities as well. People who knew him say that humility was an integral part of his character. However, Gujarmal exhibited a sense of entitlement which could border on arrogance at times. The sense of entitlement within Gujarmal Modi came less from his heritage and more from the knowledge that all his achievements could be credited to him and his work. Gujarmal Modi set up some of the finest factories with modern machinery sourced from around the world. At the same time, he deeply believed in sadhus and gurus. A rational man at most times, he would confound people by actioning something because he had dreamt about it in his sleep. A champion of women's education, he set up educational and vocational institutes for women. But he did not want women employed in any of his factories.

When Gujarmal lived with his father in Patiala, he found living in a *riyasat* (princely state) under a ruler a trifle constricting.

However, he himself lived like a ruler in Modinagar, the township he set up and owned. He did not have a royal lineage but the residents of Modinagar treated him like their king. He loved it—and even expected it! People in the town could not walk with him when he went for walks; they had to walk two steps behind him. He had left the riyasat behind, but some of the trappings of a princely state followed him to Modinagar and he adopted them, almost as if it were quite natural.

None of these contradictions, however, came in the way of his single-minded focus and determination to set up factories and mills. While he kept the women of his own and the extended family away from the core business, his brothers, nephews and sons were an integral part of the ever-expanding empire. Along with the sharp focus on the business and its profitability, Gujarmal Modi kept an equal focus on various philanthropic activities. A hard-nosed businessman, he ensured that each business contributed 10 per cent of their earnings towards the various family trusts, which used the funds to set up more than a hundred charitable projects, which included, among others, hospitals, dispensaries, schools, colleges, temples, dharamshalas and guest houses.

The story of Gujarmal Modi is instructive even for the entrepreneurs of today who often complain about the many constraints they face in setting up and then running their enterprises. As I travelled back in time along with Gujarmal Modi, it was evident that he looked at constraints not as roadblocks but as minor speed breakers. Modern-day entrepreneurs could also learn from Gujarmal Modi about the art of caring for their employees along with an absolutely strict focus on discipline. So, in reading the life story of Gujarmal Modi, the entrepreneurs of today would mostly find that hard work, determination, grit and focus go hand in hand with the spirit of entrepreneurship.

Gujarmal Modi had lived his life keeping his family together. All family members—his wife, five sons, daughters-in-law, grandchildren, brother, brother's wife, nephews and their wives—lived under the same roof. The house—Modi Mansion—kept adding new wings and rooms as the size of the family grew, but had only one kitchen. Gujarmal's credo was *'ek mukhiya, ek choolah'* (one head, one kitchen). Keeping his family together was Gujarmal's core value and deep desire. It is, therefore, a regretful irony that the family split very soon after his death. His brother and nephews wanted to go their way and the close family ties present during Gujarmal's lifetime were torn apart, very often publicly. However, today Gujarmal could take solace from one fact—even after the acrimonious splitting of the extended Modi family, his five sons and their families continue to be close. Each of his five sons has his own business; they stay separately but each one can bank on his brothers in case of any need. There are valuable lessons for family business–owners in the story of Gujarmal Modi and his business empire. His story reiterates the fact that any discord in the family is sure to affect the business negatively.

As you read this story in the following pages, you will find that my role as the author is that of a narrator. I have taken creative licence when recounting the stories of various people, their conversations and even those of Gujarmal Modi himself. Most dialogue is imagined. Some of the names used in the story are also fictitious. Many of the people in the story are no longer alive and thus the narration is based on the memories of people who interacted with them and/or the archives of the Modi family. The creative licence has been used with the objective of bringing to life the times gone by and the man that was Gujarmal Modi.

Now presenting to you Gujarmal Modi, one of the entrepreneurs who made India.

# 1

# *The Inheritor of the Legacy of Multanimal, Chiranjilal and Rambaksh Modi*

GUJARMAL Modi came from a family of businessmen and traders. In fact, his business lineage went back four generations. His great-grandfather, Rambaksh Modi, lived in Kanoud, which today is known as Mahendragarh. Back in the 1800s, Kanoud was the capital of the nawab of Jhajjar's principality. Rambaksh used to provide rations and other provisions to the nawab's army. He had good business ethics and built a stellar reputation and general goodwill in the market. The nawab, too, was happy with the integrity and diligence displayed by Rambaksh and, over the years, came to consider him a key part of his principality.

The Mutiny of 1857 resulted in a backlash against the Englishmen. Jhajjar had a couple of them posted in the principality, who came under threat from the locals during the mutiny. The nawab was responsible for their safety, and he knew that the foreigners had to be moved out of Jhajjar. He needed a trustworthy person to escort them and it fell upon Rambaksh to ensure that these men were transported safely out of danger.

It was a tricky time for Rambaksh. He was conscious of the seething anger of the Indians against the British. The mutiny was inspiring even ordinary people to rise up against the British in whatever small manner they could. In such an environment, Rambaksh was mindful of the backlash from fellow Indians if he were seen helping the British—who were now clearly the enemy of the Indians. People could call him a traitor and a collaborator. On the other hand, Rambaksh knew that his business interests were controlled by the nawab and, with one stroke of his pen, he could take away Rambaksh's lucrative business contracts. He mulled over the pros and cons of helping the nawab and the Britishers. Rambaksh was an entrepreneur and worked out a way to handle the possible negatives.

'Nawab sahib, since you have asked me personally, I will, of course, ensure that your British guests are escorted safely,' said Rambaksh as he stood in front of the nawab. He then folded his hands, bowed his head and continued speaking. 'However, sahib, I want this to remain a secret between you and me. You know my family will be lynched if others find out that I helped the white men,' Rambaksh requested. The nawab nodded his agreement.

With this promise in hand, Rambaksh worked with one of his trusted employees on the plan to get the Britishers out of Jhajjar. Rambaksh had not told any other member of his household—family or staff—about his plan. After the household had gone to sleep, he asked his employee—Saligram—to get the Britishers—Victor and Ralph—from the nawab's safekeeping. The white men were frightened because they knew that there was danger for them in Jhajjar.

The two men were taken to the outhouse that was used by Rambaksh as a storehouse. Sacks of grain were stacked higgledy-piggledy in the room without a window. When Rambaksh entered the storehouse, he found the two Britishers sitting against some sacks, fear writ large on their faces. They looked at Rambaksh apprehensively and then at the two bags in his hands.

'You are my nawab's guests and I will get you both to safety,' said Rambaksh as he set down the two bags near the Britishers. He then hitched up his dhoti and squatted on the ground as he rummaged in the bags. He took out a box of brown shoe polish and handed it to the two men.

'What do you want us to do with this?' asked Victor as he toyed with the shoe-polish box.

'You need to rub it on your face, hands and legs—any part of the body that is visible,' replied Rambaksh. 'And make sure that you get Ralph to do this also.'

Victor and Ralph looked at each other and grimaced. 'Surely you are joking, Mr Rambaksh,' said Ralph. 'Why would we put shoe polish on our body?' he continued a bit brusquely.

Rambaksh did not like Ralph's tone of voice. 'Your choice, gentlemen. You want me to help you to safety, then you do as I ask,' Rambaksh said, shrugging his shoulders.

'And after you have finished with the shoe polish, you can change out of your clothes,' he continued. He pulled out two sets of dhoti-kurta, a gamchha and a chadder and handed them over to the Britishers. 'You wear this and wait for instructions. I will come and get you once I find the time is right,' said Rambaksh.

The Britishers looked at each other and shrugged. They realized that they were at the mercy of the Indians in Jhajjar. If they wanted to get to safety, they needed to trust Rambaksh. 'Okay, we will do this, Mr Rambaksh,' said Victor.

Rambaksh knew that the middle of the afternoon was the time when most people were indoors. It was hot in the afternoons and people preferred to be inside their houses or shops. Rambaksh and Saligram used the morning to load up a bullock cart with provisions. The two Britishers were in the back of the cart, with their faces covered with the gamchhas, while Rambaksh sat in the front. His trusted employee was made to walk alongside the cart. Rambaksh told Victor and Ralph to sit facing each other and pretend to sleep. 'Whatever you do, just make sure that the chadder is wrapped around you and the gamchha covers most of your face,' instructed Rambaksh sternly.

The people of Jhajjar were used to seeing Rambaksh transport provisions for the army. As they ambled across the village, Rambaksh confidently waved to the passers-by and greeted them. *'Ram Ram, bhai, kaise ho?'* was the standard greeting Rambaksh used. The passers-by, in turn, waved back as they greeted Rambaksh with *'Ram, Ram, Rambaksh ji.'* No one suspected any foul play and Rambaksh was thus able to ensure that the Englishmen were safely escorted to Rewari.

However, during the aftermath of the mutiny, the nawab himself was defeated, and ultimately killed, by the British forces. Kanoud and Jhajjar, thus, came under British rule. Since Rambaksh had ensured the safety of the British nationals, he was seen as a person that the British could trust. And so, Rambaksh continued to supply rations to the army, which was now the British Army.

After the dust of the mutiny had settled down and the British were firmly back in control, they wanted to reward some of the Indian rulers who had helped them. One way the British did so was by handing out additional areas for them to rule. So Kanoud was handed over to the maharaja of Patiala, Mahendra Singh, who promptly changed the name of the gifted principality to Mahendragarh. However, this annexation of Kanoud by the maharaja of Patiala presented a new opportunity for Rambaksh. Under the various treaties signed by the rulers of the princely states, the riyasats had to keep a British Army and pay for their upkeep. Since Rambaksh was firmly established as a trusted supplier, he sought permission to open a new office in Patiala to supply rations to the British Army there. Permission was given with alacrity, and the business of Rambaksh Modi grew manifold.

Business continued to expand even after the death of Rambaksh Modi. The key driver of the growth and consolidation of the business was Rambaksh's son—Chiranjilal Modi. He leveraged the goodwill of his father and built closer relationships with the British soldiers. Soon cantonments stretching from Peshawar to Kanpur were supplied rations and other provisions by the Modi family. Chiranjilal even inducted his brother and nephew into the business.

Chiranjilal was a trader by profession and a bania by caste. However, he had to undergo harsh military training, which was not associated with either his profession or caste. The British Army had a condition for their ration suppliers—that they would go through the strictest military training if they wanted to remain vendors. Chiranjilal went through the training and it left a deep impact on him. The focus on discipline and processes became an integral part of his personality. His bearing changed as he grew a bushy moustache and started walking briskly and with his back ramrod straight. In later years, his grandson, Gujarmal, would follow his example of being focused on discipline.

Meanwhile, the Modi business had grown in size and spread across a larger geographical area. To manage the supplies effectively, Chiranjilal set up his headquarters in Multan with branches in Kanpur, Ambala, Nawshera and Jalandhar. Multan proved fortuitous for Chiranjilal as he was blessed with a son in 1875. As the son was born in Multan, the baby was named Multanimal. Within a couple of years of Multanimal's birth, Chiranjilal shifted his business headquarters to Patiala as the family found the climate of the city more favourable. The Modi family's connection with Kanoud, now named Mahendragarh, continued as Chiranjilal had a temple constructed there and spent money on a new park so that people could use the green area for recreation.

***

Multanimal Modi, father of Gujarmal, grew up in an environment of business and trade. He observed his father and uncles work with the British Army and provide them with various services. But he wanted to do something different—something more than just supplying rations to the British Army. Multanimal went to his father and asked for permission to start his own independent business.

'Son, I am happy that you want to do something on your own,' said Chiranjilal, 'but you will have to find the funds for it yourself. I will not give you money to start a new business.' Chiranjilal was proud of his son's entrepreneurial spirit but had wanted his progeny to continue the thriving family business. On the other hand, he also realized that his son had wider ambitions than just being a trader and did not want to come in the way of youth entrepreneurship.

Unfazed by the condition laid down by his father, Multanimal simply folded his hands, bowed his head and said, 'Thank you, father, for your permission. Your blessings are all the capital that I need.' Indeed, with the blessings of his father, young Multanimal was able to source external finance to get himself started. As he was familiar with trading, it was natural for him to explore business ideas in the trading domain. In Patiala and the areas around it were rich farmers of agricultural produce. Here Multanimal started trading in grain. Soon he became the supplier of grain for a local flour mill being run by some Parsi and Sikh businessmen. While he was happy with the steady business and the income thereof, Multanimal kept looking out for new opportunities.

The mill, which was supplied grain by Multanimal, produced atta and maida and supplied these to the big wholesalers. Multanimal saw an opportunity here and got into action. He approached the mill owners and told them that he wanted to buy quantities of atta and maida directly from them. The owners, happy with Multanimal's work, agreed. Multanimal then opened up a shop in the local bazaar and got his younger brother, Angnamal, to manage it. Thus, within a short span of time, Multanimal not only had a trading business but also a thriving retail business.

Opportunity knocked once again on Multanimal's door in the mid-1890s. The local mill owners were faced with a financial problem and were unable to pay their suppliers. Multanimal, too, was not paid for the grain he supplied. The financial problems continued, and the owners were forced to sell the mill to pay off their debts. Young Multanimal saw this as a great opportunity and put together the funds to make an offer to the mill owners. The Parsi and Sikh owners were happy to sell their business to Multanimal as they had grown fond of the young man over time.

The flour mill needed reorganization of business and production, and Multanimal understood this well. As a supplier of grain to the mill, he had built a rapport with the employees. Through the informal network he had also understood that the problem with the mill was not a serious one—the new owner only had to tweak the production and procurement systems and be more involved in the business. He actioned the new systems, and in less than a year, the flour mill was making profits once more. Besides making money for Multanimal, the turnaround of the mill also established his reputation as an astute businessman.

While his business was doing well, Multanimal was having complications in his personal life. His first wife had died after four years of marriage, after giving birth to a baby girl. Multanimal was under pressure from his family to marry again. The Modi family was an orthodox Hindu family and believed that a man needed to have a son in order to attain salvation. Young Multanimal agreed to marry again, and in 1896, he married Chandi Devi, who was the daughter of a local businessman. The wishes of the family bore fruit, and in 1902, Multanimal and Chandi Devi were blessed with a baby boy. The entire family was ecstatic as, finally, an heir had been born to the Modi family. This boy would grow up to be Gujarmal Modi.

Gujarmal came into the world bringing great joy to the family. This joy, however, turned into sorrow as Chandi Devi died within a week of giving birth to Gujarmal. The happiness of the family turned to concern as the baby had to be looked after. The family needed to find a wet nurse who would feed the baby. They located one in the village of Majra and brought her over to live in the Modi home. The wet nurse was called Gujari, and so everyone started calling the baby Gujar. In Indian families, till a formal name is given at the naam-karan ceremony, newborn babies are called by pet names. Gujar became the baby's pet name.

As the baby and the wet nurse settled down, Multanimal organized a big naam-karan ceremony for his son. After the yagna, the priest named the baby Ram Prasad. But the name Gujar had stuck on everyone's lips, and the baby's nickname became his official name. As he grew older, Gujarmal made no attempt to get people to call him by his given name either. It is providential that in later years when Gujarmal attained his fame, it was the name of his wet nurse that also gained recognition.

Eventually, as Gujarmal was settled with his wet nurse, Multanimal was persuaded by his family to marry once more. He did, but that wife, too, died, within a year of marriage. Multanimal married a fourth time, and this marriage endured. His fourth marriage was to Rukmini Devi, who was the daughter of a rich businessman in Mahendragarh. Gujarmal was only two-and-a-half years old when Rukmini Devi came into the Modi house as his stepmother. It was Rukmini Devi who brought up Gujarmal, and his elder sister, Sundari Devi (born of Multanimal's first wife), as her own children. Rukmini Devi and Multanimal had three sons and three daughters over the years. All through his life, Gujarmal, too, looked upon Rukmini Devi as his mother.

'Gujarmal, I know that everyone looks at me as your stepmother,' said Rukmini Devi as she sat combing young Gujarmal's hair. 'But I promise you that I will be more than your mother. No one will be able to say that I love anyone more than I love you,' she continued. Gujarmal, all of three years old, did not understand fully what his mother was saying. All he knew was that he was the apple of his mother's eye. He turned and hugged Rukmini Devi.

Rukmini Devi was to have an overarching influence in shaping Gujarmal. Though she was aware that she was Multanimal's fourth wife and Gujarmal's stepmother, and sure that she would have children of her own, she did not want to be seen as the stereotypical stepmother and, thus, overcompensated by way of her affection for Gujarmal. As the eldest son of Multanimal, Gujarmal had a special place in his father's heart and everyone knew that Gujarmal was his favourite child. To add to this, Gujarmal became the focus of his stepmother's love and care as well. She encouraged him from childhood and gave him the belief that he would get far in life.

A person's life is shaped by his childhood. Gujarmal's was spent with parents who, in their individual manner, gave him the confidence that he could accomplish anything that he set his mind to. Later in his life, Gujarmal was to meet another woman who would have a strong impact on his life—his wife, who took on from where Rukmini Devi left off. Under the influence of two strong women, Gujarmal was destined to succeed and achieve big things in his life.

# 2

# *A High School Dropout*

'GUJARMAL, I want you to drop out of school,' said Multanimal as he leaned back in his chair.

It was an evening in Patiala, and the lamps were being lit by the servants in the Modi home. Multanimal had returned from his office but was yet to change into the more comfortable kurta-pyjama. He was dressed in his achkan and churidar, with a vibrant-coloured safa on his head. His wife had given him a glass of tea and he took a large swig as he continued talking to his son. 'There is no point in you waiting another year to clear high school.'

Gujarmal's face fell. He was sitting cross-legged on the floor and he lowered his face so that his father could not see his disappointment. He kept quiet. The silence was broken by the loud chirping of the birds as they prepared to settle down in the trees.

'So, you agree, Gujarmal?' asked Multanimal as he took another sip of the tea.

Gujarmal looked up and his eyes were moist with unshed tears. His seventeenth birthday was a few months away. 'But, father, why should I drop out of school? I want to study more,' he said softly. 'And you do know, don't you, that it is not my fault that the fees for the exams were not paid?' he added.

'Whatever it is, you cannot take the exam this year, can you?' asked Multanimal brusquely.

Gujarmal only shook his head slowly in answer.

'So, if you want to clear high school, you will have to take the exam next year? Right?' continued Multanimal.

Gujarmal nodded reluctantly.

'My son, do you really want to spend another year learning lessons you already know? Isn't that a complete waste of time?' thundered Multanimal. 'Complete waste of time, I say! Total waste.' He continued, shaking his head, 'You are better off joining me in the business. You know that I cannot handle it all on my own.'

Gujarmal's face reflected his dilemma. He was brought up in a household where the father's word was the absolute law. He knew that he could not go against his father's wishes. But he was also aware of the deep affection and love Multanimal had for him. Gujarmal decided to focus on the love and said, 'Father, you know that I will obey your every wish. But you also know that I want to go to university to study more after high school. I want to learn more. Please, father, I really want to study.'

But Multanimal's mind was made up. 'Son, you have studied till high school and that is enough for a businessman,' he said. And then his face softened as he looked at his eldest son with kindness. 'I promise you, son, that I will find ways for you to get an education in business-specific studies,' he said as he bent down and ruffled his son's hair.

Gujarmal closed his eyes as he felt his father's hand on his head and a strange peace came over him. His instinct told him that he should accept the decision without rancour. Gujarmal raised his hand, caught his father's and brought it to his own heart. 'Father, I will do what you wish. You have my promise that I will give the business my full focus,' he said.

Multanimal was delighted. 'Son, you will not regret this. I am sure of it,' he said. And then he turned reflective. 'I still remember the day I took you to the maulvi's class when you were four years old. Even then you wanted to learn more.' He laughed at the memory.

***

Indeed, Gujarmal's formal education had started at the age of four, when he had been enrolled in a home-study class run by a maulvi in the locality. Gujarmal had grown up in a family that was not only wealthy but also respected by the local community. The Modi house was always open to visitors, who sometimes came just to chat and at other times to seek advice. The large courtyard had charpoys and moodhas strewn around for visitors, and hot tea was kept bubbling on the choolah, ready to be served. It was not unusual to see Chiranjilal sitting on a charpoy surrounded by some men from the community, who had come to seek advice, while their children ran around in the courtyard. Sometimes the children would also be asked to sit down and listen to Chiranjilal's tales about the value of discipline. The Modi household was a busy household. Multanimal and Chiranjilal had earned enormous goodwill in society and the business communities due to their work.

India in the early twentieth century, under the British rule, was an orthodox society, but the value of education was recognized. Thus, when Gujarmal had turned four years old, Multanimal looked around for a school for him.

It would be prudent to note here that in the early 1900s, there were no nursery schools; there were only government and private schools for older children and colleges for higher education. However, the Indian entrepreneurial class had found a way to address the need for younger children to learn. It was a variation of the modern-day tuition culture. In the years when Gujarmal was growing up, it was common to find teachers, priests and maulvis to teach young children at home. Most of the time this was done without any monetary payment. The teachers were happy, instead, to receive food and other household items as dakshina (charity) from their students.

Multanimal found one such maulvi near his house and enrolled Gujarmal in that class. The maulvi taught the Mahajani style of writing, among other subjects. The Mahajani script was a mercantile script that had been historically used in the northern part of undivided India for writing accounts and other financial records (the word 'mahajan' is Hindi for 'banker'). Multanimal wanted his son to learn Mahajani as he believed it would come in useful in later years, as it did. Gujarmal, even at that age, showed an inclination towards numbers and went to the maulvi enthusiastically. Very soon, he became proficient in the Mahajani script.

Gujarmal's grandfather, Chiranjilal, was the patriarch of the Modi family and it was natural for Multanimal to ask him for advice regarding Gujarmal's education. It was under his grandfather's guidance that the young boy was enrolled in a government school when he was six years old.

All through his childhood, Gujarmal was influenced by his parents and his grandfather. Chiranjilal had undergone military training when he had expanded his business to cater to the British army. As a result, he was focused on discipline and punctuality. Gujarmal grew up in this atmosphere, and discipline became an integral part of his life. In fact, Chiranjilal was very keen that his first grandson also join the military school and become an army officer. If he had lived longer, it is possible that Chiranjilal would have seen Gujarmal become a general in the army. Fate had other plans, however. In 1913, Chiranjilal died unexpectedly and his dream of his first grandson joining the army remained just that. The army's loss was to be the business world's gain in the years to follow.

Besides his grandfather, his grandmother and mother, too, left a deep impression on his upbringing. From the women of the Modi household, Gujarmal learnt the value of religion and spirituality. Rukmini Devi would tell stories to Gujarmal every evening. These stories focused on the values of being fair to people and doing good in life.

'Remember, Gujarmal, don't be weak. Fight when you have to. But don't start a fight,' Rukmini Devi would say again and again. She would also teach him the merits of hard work. 'Never take wealth for granted, my son,' she would say. 'You are fortunate to be born in a rich family, but this is all transitory. We could lose all our money one day. Never bank on this money. Always work hard and create your own wealth,' Rukmini Devi would teach him repeatedly. She also gave him examples from the Ramayana and the Mahabharata about princes having to live like ascetics. 'Don't get so used to these good things in life that you lose the ability to live without them,' she reminded Gujarmal often.

But mostly she kept encouraging him to be a karma-yogi. Karma yoga is one of the three spiritual paths in Hinduism and is based on the yoga of action. A karma-yogi looks at the right action as a form of prayer. 'You will go far, Gujarmal, if you follow karma yoga and not accumulate wealth only for your personal gain. Be sure to use your wealth for the welfare of others as well,' was the lesson that Rukmini Devi gave Gujarmal every day. These informal lessons from his mother stayed with Gujarmal, forming his character and influencing his actions all through his life.

Besides the stories from his mother, there were sessions of bhajans every day in the house and Gujarmal sat through them all as he did when the priest would give discourses on the Ramayana. The women kept weekly fasts to honour various devi-devtaas (gods) and occasionally Gujarmal, too, would observe the fast along with his mother and grandmother. When it came to the fast for Janmashtami, he was at the forefront. This fast is a tough fast as one is not supposed to have anything to eat or drink. Instead of finding ways to hide and sip water, Gujarmal ensured that not only he but no one else who was fasting could sneak away to have an occasional sip. These childhood influences informed his later life and, along with discipline, religion and spirituality remained integral to him.

Religion and spirituality went hand in hand with philanthropy, as Gujarmal learnt from his father, Multanimal. He had observed the various actions of his father, not limited to the setting up of a Sanatan Dharam school in Patiala or of gaushalas (cow shelters). Gujarmal saw his father spend time helping people and keeping aside part of the wealth generated towards charitable activities. Even the spiritual discourses in the evening at the Modi home focused on the benefits of philanthropy. It was said that helping the needy hastened the process of achieving nirvana. Being deeply influenced by the religious and spiritual talks, Gujarmal decided to commit small acts of generosity himself.

As a young pre-teenager, Gujarmal would get two paise per day as his pocket money. The pocket money was to meet the daily need of buying ink to write and the remainder was to be spent on street food after school. Gujarmal, however, put into action the learnings from observing his father. After spending money to buy ink for himself, he would use the remainder to buy either books or ink for the less fortunate students of his school. He had started doing these small philanthropic deeds so that he could go back and proudly tell his mother about them. Soon he discovered that helping others gave him a great sense of joy. Gujarmal felt fulfilled and, in some ways, less guilty for being better off than many others. Over time, these deeds that were small to start with grew in size as Gujarmal himself grew as a person and a businessman.

One other habit that was imbibed early in his life through his grandfather was staying focused on health. Chiranjilal had instilled in the young boy respect for a healthy body and the need for regular exercise. This was reiterated by Rukmini Devi, who encouraged her son to be strong in mind and in body. She gave him a tall glass of milk brimming with malai every morning, along with almonds that had been soaked through the night. Both Chiranjilal and Rukmini Devi encouraged Gujarmal to do various physical exercises. Even as a young child, Gujarmal would spend time on kushti (wrestling) and body-building. As a teenager he was a tall youngster and already towered over his father. With all the physical exercise he did, he had the appearance of a wrestler. The Modi household was strictly vegetarian and Gujarmal, too, spent his life as one. He also was a teetotaller.

***

Gujarmal's grandfather had passed away in 1913 when the young boy was eleven years old. Chiranjilal had had two dreams—one, for his grandson to join the army, and the other, for him to get married. The first dream remained unfulfilled, but the second dream of his grandfather was fulfilled in a couple of years. At the age of thirteen, Gujarmal was married to Rajban Devi, daughter of Seth Govardhan Das of a village in Rajasthan. It was not uncommon for child marriages to take place in India in the early twentieth century. Though it was banned by a law passed in 1929, the unlawful practice was prevalent later and continues even in current times in some parts of India. But in 1915 it was legal, and it was common for young boys, especially boys belonging to wealthy families, to get married. Thus, Gujarmal got married as a teen but his child bride continued to stay at her parents' home as this was also the practice. The gaunaa, or departure of the bride to her in-laws' house, took place after a couple of years. Gujarmal's studies continued uninterrupted even after the wedding ceremony and he looked forward to joining a college or a university after his high school. But fate had other plans for the boy.

Gujarmal was in the last year of high school and was preparing for the annual exams. He was already making plans with some friends about going to college to study further. It was the summer season and the days were hot and dusty. One day, the high school students were on their way to their classes when the sky was shrouded in dark clouds and it started raining. The temperature dropped and the day turned cool with a pleasant breeze blowing. As they were walking towards their class, the students met their maths teacher.

'It is such a pleasant day, children. Do you really want to sit in a classroom and study?' asked the maths teacher. The students looked at each other and shook their heads. 'Good,' said the teacher. 'I propose that we take the rest of the day off and go for a hike. It would be such a shame to waste a beautiful day by sitting indoors,' he continued.

The boys all whooped with joy as a day spent in nature was preferable to a day spent doing equations. They passed the day hiking through the local woods. But this day of loafing resulted in unpleasantness for the boys. They did not know that the headmaster of their school had a personal enmity with the maths teacher. The headmaster used the day of hiking to level a charge against the maths teacher. A charge was made that the teacher had instigated the students to boycott classes and engineered a mini revolt against the school. Loud and vehement denials by the students fell on deaf ears. The headmaster was determined to take action against the teacher. The students were collateral damage.

As the matter involved a senior teacher and almost the entire class, it was treated seriously by the supervisory board of the school. They set up an inquiry committee and after the report was presented, the board concluded that it was the students who were at fault. The board also said that the students needed to apologize to the board and the headmaster.

As the students heard about the decision of the board, they were upset as they believed it was not their fault. Gujarmal was looked upon as the class leader and the group gathered around him as they discussed among themselves what to do next. Gujarmal himself was very upset at this ruling of the board.

His sense of fair play and justice was offended. He believed, rightly so, that the students were not at fault. He told his fellow students that he would appeal to the board.

The board convened again and Gujarmal presented the case of the students. Using logic and his articulation skills, he proved to the board that the students were innocent. Now the board was in a dilemma. Overruling their earlier verdict would show the members of the board in a bad light. However, asking the students to apologize when they were not at fault would be unfair to the students. The board, unwilling to overrule its own decision, took the easy way out and referred the matter to the court of the maharaja of Patiala.

The drama continued in the maharaja's court. The students were so focused on this real-life drama that all of them forgot that the date of fee submission for their final exams had passed! By the time the students realized this, it was too late. Since they would not be able to take their final exams, they would all have to repeat the year.

Multanimal did not want his son, Gujarmal, to waste a year repeating a grade in school. He told Gujarmal to drop out of school and join him in the business. The business had been expanding rapidly, especially after the start of the First World War. The demand for supplies to the British Army had increased manifold and Multanimal needed a trusted assistant to help him manage the business.

Gujarmal was not happy at all at the thought of dropping out of school. 'Father, I want to study more, and I do want to go to university. Please don't ask me to drop out of school,' he pleaded with Multanimal.

'Son, you have studied till Class Ten and that is enough for a businessman. If you want to study more, I will find ways for you to be educated in business-specific studies,' said Multanimal decisively.

Gujarmal was brought up in a household where the father's word was law. Gujarmal bowed to his father's wishes and joined him in the business. However, he held his father to his word and got him to arrange private tuition at home. Multanimal, true to his word, got his son to study the bahi-khata management using the Mahajani script, accountancy and the principles of business. To supplement his academic learning, Gujarmal was told to start work as a munim (treasurer) at one of the shops of the family.

Dropping out of school and getting into the family business was the turning point in Gujarmal's life. He did not look back after that.

# 3

# *Learning Life Lessons on the Job*

GUJARMAL had been working with his father for some time now. Initially the workers and staff at the office treated him like a child even though he was nearing his twentieth birthday—after all, they had seen him grow up literally in front of their eyes! But, very soon, Gujarmal carved out a space for himself within the business. People who interacted with him walked away with a sense of having dealt with someone whose business vision belied his young age.

This vision and maturity had been learnt the hard way by Gujarmal. His father was a good teacher and had his own way of teaching his son the lessons of business.

When Gujarmal had just joined the business and started working in the flour mill, he found that the price charged for maida was the highest in the market. He asked his father about it.

'Our quality is the best, son, and that is why people pay us the premium,' said Multanimal.

Gujarmal kept it in mind as he continued working. Accounts and numbers were his strengths. He did some back-of-the-envelope calculations and found that a slight increase in productivity at the mill would lead to a much higher profit. Gujarmal looked at the process of producing maida more keenly to find out how he could increase productivity.

'Father, I have found a way to increase our profitability,' exclaimed Gujarmal one evening as he met his father at home at dinner time. When asked for details, Gujarmal explained that he would increase the size of the holes of the screens used to sift the maida at the final stage of production. 'It will be such a small increase that no one will notice it, father,' Gujarmal explained eagerly. 'But the quantity of maida that we will produce because of this will increase by 20 per cent. That means 20 per cent higher profits,' he continued and looked at his father triumphantly.

The father looked at his son and smiled indulgently. 'Gujarmal, you are running the business. If you want to do it, go ahead and learn the lesson yourself,' said Multanimal. 'But remember there is a reason that people pay us a premium for our maida. It is because of our quality,' he added gently.

'Oh, father, no one will notice,' exclaimed Gujarmal. 'I don't know why you did not realize this earlier. Now watch as I increase the profits of the mill.' Multanimal merely smiled quietly and went on eating his food.

Gujarmal changed the screens in the process of the final sifting of maida. There were no adverse comments from the buyers in the initial month. However, within a couple of months, the orders started going down as people complained about the quality. Gujarmal watched dejectedly as the profits of the mill started falling. He realized what his father had tried to tell him. He directed the restoration of the original screens immediately, but the orders took more than a year to come back to their original amounts.

'Father, I have learnt my lesson,' said Gujarmal one evening as he sat with his father. 'I have learnt that we cannot compromise on our quality. I will never forget this lesson in my life—that the trust of the people cannot be broken.' This lesson was to stay with him all through his life, even when the Modi Group became one of the top ten in India.

***

The World War in the early twentieth century had caused many a logistical problem for the transportation of goods within undivided India. The local mills of Patiala had to transport their products like atta, maida and sooji by bullock carts to Ambala, Amritsar and even Lahore. The mill owners had a twin problem due to this form of transportation. One was that it took a long time to transport the food products. The other problem was the fact that the mill owners had to pay a cess which was calculated per sack carried in the bullock carts. As was evident, it increased the cost of the products, making them uncompetitive in the market.

When Gujarmal was confronted with the problem of transporting the products of his mill, he delved into its various aspects. As part of his research, he found that there was a mill in Ambala that was transporting its atta and maida by train to various cities, including Lahore and Amritsar. The cost of rail transport worked out better as there was no cess to be paid per sack of flour and the train was faster than the bullock carts.

As a result, the Ambala flour mill could transport more at less costs and, thus, earn a bigger profit. Gujarmal wanted to find out more about the mill and the mill owner.

'Have you heard about this Chawla who runs a mill in Ambala?' asked Gujarmal as he sat in the local market, sipping tea. There were four other men there taking a break from work.

'Oh, that Chawla? The one who sends his stuff by rail?' said Manraj, one of the men there, as he waved his hand dismissively. The hand he waved was the one holding the tea glass. The other men around him ducked instinctively, fearing the hot tea being splashed on them.

'Yes, that Chawla,' confirmed Gujarmal. 'Do you know how he manages to do this?'

Manraj put down his tea glass and beckoned Gujarmal towards him. The other men also moved nearer as they did not want to miss out on what Manraj had to say.

Gujarmal came closer to Manraj who, leaning in, started speaking in a conspiratorial tone. 'You know, Chawla is a great friend of the governor sahib,' began Manraj.

'Which governor sahib are you talking about?' butted in Tanvir, one of the other three men.

'Arrey, the governor of Punjab. Which other governor do you think I am talking about?' Manraj said in an irritated manner as he did not like Tanvir interrupting him. 'Now be quiet and listen,' he said firmly.

Everyone looked at Tanvir and gestured for him to be quiet. They all wanted to hear what Manraj had to say.

'So, Chawla and governor sahib are friends. You know, Chawla goes to the governor's house and has tea with him when he goes to Lahore,' said Manraj. 'It is because of this friendship that Chawla is allowed to use the railway wagon network to transport his stuff. Lucky man this Chawla.'

'How can this be?' asked Gujarmal. 'I don't believe it. I don't think it is that simple.'

'If you don't believe me, ask anyone else in this city. Everyone knows this,' said Manraj brusquely as he got up, irritated that Gujarmal was questioning him. He hitched up his dhoti, gave a nod to the others and stomped off.

Gujarmal asked other people in the local trader community about Chawla using the trains to transport his products. What he heard seemed to corroborate Manraj's statements. He was told that ordinary people could not use the train wagons to transport products. When he asked about the mill owner in Ambala, he was told that the owner indeed had a deep friendship with the governor of Punjab and thus was allowed to use the rail wagons to transport his products.

Gujarmal could not digest this fact. As a young man, he was tall, strapping and well-built. Further, he had studied till high school and was knowledgeable about matters of trade and commerce. He had been brought up by parents who told him that he was second to none. He believed that he, too, could get the same deal as Chawla, the mill owner. 'If that ordinary mill owner in Ambala can be friends with the governor of Punjab, why should I not try to at least have a business association with the governor?' thought Gujarmal. He told himself that he did not want an abiding friendship with the governor but just an acquaintanceship so that he, too, could avail of the rail wagon facility to transport his products to other cities.

'Father, I want to go to Lahore to meet the governor of Punjab,' said Gujarmal as he met his father in the evening at dinner time.

'Why this sudden desire to go to Lahore, son?' asked Multanimal as he took a bite of his roti.

Gujarmal explained to his father the logistical problem and how he wanted to go to meet the governor or even someone in the governor's office to get permission to transport goods by rail.

'But why do you think that the governor or his office will even talk to a young man like yourself?' Multanimal wondered aloud as he burped gently after a good meal.

'Father, you still look upon me as a child.' Gujarmal smiled as he looked at his father fondly. 'But look at me. Really *look* at me. Am I not taller than you? The others don't treat me as a child, you know.' He continued to smile as he spoke to his father.

'All right, all right. You are an old man.' Multanimal laughed as he gently patted his son on the head. 'Okay, go to Lahore and try your luck, but be careful how you talk to people in the governor's office.'

Gujarmal was delighted and jumped up immediately. Multanimal extended his hand and held Gujarmal. 'Where are you running off to, my boy? What is the rush? I said you can go but you have to take an older person with you, Gujarmal. Why don't you ask Gopal Shah to accompany you?' he suggested.

Gopal Shah was a family loyalist who worked as a munim with the Modi family. Gujarmal agreed and both men went off to Lahore to find a way to access the rail wagon network for their products.

Once they reached Lahore, Gujarmal decided to first visit the railway office before trying to meet anyone in the governor's office. He was directed to the department that dealt with transport and the wagons. Gujarmal explained the problem to the railway officers and also told them of the Ambala mill owner who exploited his friendship with the governor of Punjab to use the rail wagon network. 'I do not claim to be a friend or even an acquaintance of the governor, but I do want to find a way to use the rail wagon network for transporting my goods,' said Gujarmal with a smile.

As they heard about the Ambala mill owner, the railway officers looked at each other in surprise. And then they heard Gujarmal ask them about the rail wagon network. 'But no one needs to be a friend or even an acquaintance of governor sahib to use the rail wagon network,' said the older railway officer. 'All it requires is some paperwork and certification, which I am sure that you, even without your friendship with governor sahib, will be able to manage,' the officer continued with a broad smile.

'Really! I can also use the railway wagon network? You're sure?' asked Gujarmal in a rush, as if he could not believe it.

The officers looked at each other again and smiled indulgently. They liked the earnest young man in front of them. 'Of course, you can also use it,' said the younger officer.

'Young man, now do you want to go to governor sahib's residence to try to be his friend?' The older officer laughed.

Gujarmal took the ribbing in his stride. He smiled, thanked the officers and saluted them laughingly as he left. The paperwork and the certification process took a couple of days. Armed with the certificates, Gujarmal and Gopal Shah made their way home.

'Father, I have done it!' cried Gujarmal as he bent down to touch his father's feet upon reaching home. 'Now even we can use the rail wagon network to transport our goods to all cities.' Multanimal was amazed at the entrepreneurship of his son. He kissed Gujarmal on the head and blessed him.

Using the certificates, the Modi mills were able to transport their products via the rail wagon network. It resulted in reduced costs and higher turnover, which led to increased profits. Gujarmal's reputation in the trader market went up and he was seen by the others as a young man who was unfazed by any problem.

Multanimal started sharing a larger part of the burden of his work with his eldest son. However, he was mindful of the fact that Gujarmal had wanted to study more. Now that his son was totally immersed in work, Multanimal did not want to send him off to faraway lands for further studies. But he did understand his son's desire for knowledge. He found a way out to handle this for his son.

Punjab National Bank had a branch in the city and Multanimal used to deal with the bank officials for his trade and other work. He requested the branch manager to spend time with his son for a couple of hours each day to teach him bank-related transactions as well as the British procedures of accounting. 'My son knows all about the Mahajani script and the bahi-khata system. But I want him to learn the accounting system being used by others in the world,' said Multanimal. The bank manager was only too happy to oblige one of his valued clients. The manager also wanted to spend time with, and get to know better, the young man being talked about in the trading community. Gujarmal, of course, was the happiest as he moved one step forward in his quest for more knowledge.

***

As he kept his focus on learning and the actual business, Gujarmal did not lose his connection with the spiritual and religious side of his personality. There were bhajan sessions each day at home and he made sure that he was there to be a part of each of them. Discipline, too, continued to be his primary trait. All the people who worked with him and for him realized that their boss did not like people being unpunctual and got angry if people did not follow rules. Gujarmal had a quick temper but he did not bear grudges in his heart. He had a quiet confidence about himself and did not think he was inferior to anyone else. This characteristic allowed him to interact and deal with people many years older than him. He had started working very early and had to interact with staff who were much older than him. These interactions taught him lessons in the use of tact when dealing with people.

Gujarmal also continued his focus on physical wellness. As a twenty-year-old, he was over six feet tall and built like a wrestler. In fact, wrestling was one of his passions and he often called out to people to settle their differences with him in the akhara. He was surprised that not too many people took up that offer! Philanthropy, too, continued to be an integral part of the Modi family. Sometimes it got them into trouble as well.

India in the early twentieth century was dependent on the import of foodgrains to feed its people. Wheat was imported from Australia and the landed cost used to be about 4.5 ser per rupee (1 ser used to be about 4.2 kilograms). The Modi shop used a differential price for their wholesale and retail rates. Contrary to normal practice, Gujarmal would charge a higher price in the wholesale trade. The average retail customer was able to buy 5 ser of wheat per rupee from the Modi shop. The wholesale price, including to the military, was 4 ser per rupee. Gujarmal had instituted this pricing system as he believed that the institutional buyers could afford to subsidize the retail consumers.

In early 1922, a new colonel took charge at the local cantonment. The new officer took a review of all areas under his command. The Modi family was still the main supplier of food and other provisions to the army. As he reviewed the purchases, the colonel saw the price being charged by Modi Mills for wheat flour. One of the junior officers told the colonel that Modi Mills charged the army more than they charged their local retail customers.

The colonel got angry. He did not like the fact that the average Indian customer was getting wheat flour cheaper than the British Army. Gujarmal was summoned by the colonel and instructed to reduce the price. Gujarmal refused.

'But how can you refuse, Gujarmal?' shouted the British colonel. 'You know how much wheat flour we buy from you? Even then you charge me 20 per cent more than what you charge that local fellow who comes to your shop? This is unacceptable to us. Stop this and give us a cheaper rate than what you charge them,' the colonel continued to rage.

'I will not be able to do this,' said Gujarmal calmly.

'But why?' asked the colonel, completely perplexed.

'You see, when I sell at a cheaper price to the poor retail customer, I am actually doing something good for them. They cannot afford to pay more, but you can,' explained Gujarmal.

The British colonel lost his cool completely when he heard this. 'You mean to say that you are charging the British Army more to feed the poor locals? This is completely unacceptable. And philanthropy? What philanthropy are you talking about? With the amount we buy, you people are simply profiteering and making more money in the garb of religion and philanthropy,' the colonel shouted.

Gujarmal was upset at the words used by the officer. He knew that the colonel was a white man and had a higher status in society than the native Indians. He chafed against this knowledge as he had grown up believing that he was second to none. However, he kept his cool and tried to talk to the colonel in a rational manner. 'Such words do not sound good coming from the mouth of an officer,' said Gujarmal.

Unfazed, the colonel said that his philanthropy and religion were a sham and the Modis simply wanted to get richer. Till then, Gujarmal had been keeping his emotions in check. However, when he heard the colonel rubbish the Hindu religion and its associated philanthropy, Gujarmal, too, lost his temper. Heated words were exchanged between the colonel and Gujarmal. As the argument got more intense, the colonel threatened to get Gujarmal's contract cancelled.

By this time, the other officers, including some of the Indian clerks, gathered around the two men and took them aside. The colonel was counselled to speak to Gujarmal's father, which he did. Multanimal, a well-respected man in the city, listened to the complaint of the colonel and then asked his son for his comments. As he heard his son, Multanimal realized that the famed temper of Gujarmal had gotten the better of him. However, he also did not appreciate the words spoken by the colonel about the Modi family using the garb of philanthropy to enrich themselves. Multanimal was a wise man and knew that he could not afford to antagonize the British colonel. Using all the tact available to him, Multanimal defused the situation.

However, this incident enraged Gujarmal. 'How can I live in a riyasat where I can be insulted and treated like a slave?' he fumed. 'I would rather go and live somewhere else,' threatened Gujarmal. It took tact and some emotional blackmail by

Multanimal to calm his son down. But the incident and the treatment by the British colonel was not forgotten by Gujarmal.

Multanimal was aware of the deep resentment borne by Gujarmal against the colonel and wanted to somehow get his son's mind away to other matters. An opportunity presented itself in the form of a fraudulent trade transaction. What had happened was that a few weeks earlier, a well-dressed and well-spoken man had presented himself at Multanimal's office. The man, named Sahu, had presented his credentials as a respected trader of Calcutta. He said that he had heard about the Modi family even in Calcutta and wanted to meet them. Sahu further said that he wanted some advice on the Patiala and other markets as he wanted to expand his trading activities beyond Calcutta. Multanimal liked the overall demeanour of Sahu and offered him tea and refreshments. As they talked about Sahu's desire to expand, the conversation turned to the trading business of the Modi family. Sahu asked if the Modi family had trading partners in Calcutta. When he heard that the Modi business was focused in northern India, Sahu offered to help Multanimal set up trading in the Calcutta market.

Multanimal was tempted to expand geographically as by now he was trading in many food items. Sahu offered his help to sell a consignment of red chillies in the eastern region of the country. He also said that he would take care of all the paperwork. Multanimal was swept away by the enthusiasm and earnestness of Sahu. The two men agreed that the first consignment of red chillies would be sent to Calcutta by train and the bill of lading would be sent to the Calcutta trader. Sahu would give the hundi to the bank, which could be encashed by Multanimal once the goods were received in Calcutta. The hundi system was an informal bill of exchange and was basically a paper document promising payment of cash at a later time at a particular place.

The consignment was sent through the rail wagon network and then Multanimal waited to encash the hundi. But the bank did not receive any instructions nor any cash in the account of the trader. After some time, it became clear to Multanimal that he had been cheated by the well-dressed man who had masqueraded as a trader.

As he debated what action to take, Gujarmal offered to go to Calcutta to try to locate the trader and get the payment from him. The idea to go to Calcutta had come to Gujarmal in a dream. He was a great believer in dreams and would pay heed to what he had dreamt. The family was used to hearing about Gujarmal's dreams and Multanimal did not find it odd. He was sceptical, however, as Gujarmal was only twenty years old at that time, but he also saw this as an opportunity to get his son's mind off the matter of the British colonel. He agreed and Gujarmal went to Calcutta.

Gujarmal found Calcutta a thriving and busy city. He loved the hustle-bustle of the trading area. Much as he wanted to spend time in the trading market, he focused on the job at hand. He went to the railway office, met with the railway officers and told them the story of the fraud. He wanted the officers to give him the address details of the place where the consignment of red chillies was delivered. The railway officers, as is normal with bureaucrats, did not want to get involved in the matter. But Gujarmal was determined to find Sahu and get his money back.

Gujarmal threatened the railway officers that he would take them to court and charge them personally in the matter of the fraud. The officers were bureaucrats after all and did not want to be dragged into court cases. They gave the delivery address to Gujarmal.

Armed with the address, Gujarmal went to Sahu's office. The trader was flabbergasted to see Gujarmal standing in front of him. Sahu was a short, wiry man of slim build. Gujarmal was a tall and muscular man. Further, he had a booming voice. He used his voice to the fullest as he threatened Sahu with dire consequences. Gujarmal was insistent on receiving the payment as his sense of fair play had been offended. He could not understand how anyone could take the material and then refuse to pay. Whether it was the threat of the court or that Sahu was intimidated by the size of Gujarmal, he made the full payment and swore that he would not venture towards Patiala again.

Once he accomplished his mission, Gujarmal went about exploring the city. Calcutta was a thriving trading centre under British India and people from across the country came to the city to trade and conduct business. Gujarmal explored the markets and the manufacturing units. His inherent thirst for knowledge led him from one unit to the other. While he was in the market area, he saw the notice board of an insurance company. This was a word—insurance—that he had never heard earlier. He went inside the office, met the officer there and asked to know more about insurance. The officer, sensing a business opportunity, explained the concept of insurance in great detail. Gujarmal was fascinated to know that by paying a relatively small amount (the premium), all the factories of the Modi family could be insured against fire, flooding and other damage. Without wasting any time, he initiated the paperwork to get the mill in Patiala insured.

Multanimal, however, did not understand the concept of insurance at all. In fact, he was upset about the money Gujarmal had spent to pay the premium. Now it was Gujarmal's turn to become the teacher and he explained it as patiently to his father as the insurance officer had explained it to him. Finally, Multanimal grudgingly agreed that spending money for the premium had been prudent.

The trip to Calcutta turned out to be providential for Gujarmal. In 1923, almost a year and a half after his visit to Calcutta, the Modi mill in Patiala caught fire. It was a tremendous fire and engulfed everything within. However, since the mill and the material had been insured, the financial loss for the Modi family was minimal. Gujarmal's belief in messages received in his dreams became stronger. He believed that had he not gone to Calcutta following his dream, he would not have known about the insurance company and got the mill insured, and then the fire would have resulted in a major loss.

Gujarmal took charge of rebuilding the mill once the claims were settled with the insurance company. He wanted to build the new mill with the newer technology that was now available. However, he needed an able engineer to help him in the planning and execution. He located an old, loyal employee, Bhanu Kumar Mathur, an engineer who had retired in 1916 and was now living in Delhi. Gujarmal asked Multanimal to reach out to Bhanu Mathur and ask him to come back for a short consultation assignment.

Bhanu Mathur, however, was unwilling to give up his quiet life and kept declining the generous offers made by Multanimal. Finally, after much persuasion, Bhanu Mathur said that he could consider taking the offer but would work only with Gujarmal. The engineer may have thought that Multanimal and Gujarmal would not agree to the condition but, to his surprise, both agreed. In fact, Gujarmal ensured that he was with Bhanu Mathur right from the time of their morning walk and then spent the day working under his instructions. Bhanu Mathur was deaf and thus all communication had to be written. Though tedious, this helped Gujarmal build a set of detailed notes on the construction of the mill. These notes became a sort of guidebook for Gujarmal as he built many more factories and mills later in life.

Supervising and taking charge of the new mill became Gujarmal's passion, and he spent sixteen to eighteen hours each day working on the site. It also became an opportunity for him to hone his people management skills. There were over 500 workers employed for the construction of the new mill. Managing these workers and getting them to give their best taught him the basics of marrying discipline with empathy. Getting up at 5 a.m. and going for an hour-long walk became a habit which was to stay with him throughout his life. There was a reason that he worked with this zeal. It was his belief that a factory should not take more than nine months to be constructed and running. 'If a human child can be conceived and born within nine months, then why can't a factory?' was the logic he used whenever anyone asked him. Under the supervision of Bhanu Mathur and Gujarmal, the new mill was ready and launched—all within nine months. Multanimal was so happy with this progress that he made Gujarmal the general manager in charge of the mill.

The new mill had been built with modern technology and Gujarmal believed that their traditional trade practices also needed to change. The traders in the market, traditionally, quoted different rates to different buyers through the day.

The quoted rate depended on the ability of the buyer to pay and also on the competitive pricing in the market at that time. Gujarmal found this practice tedious and observed that people were frequently forced to lie when it came to settling prices. During his interactions with the British traders, he learnt that they followed the practice of one rate for one day. A rate would be fixed for the day and then all trades, whether the market for that commodity was up or down, would take place at that fixed rate. Gujarmal found this practice useful and he wanted to institute it for his business.

However, his own munims, the accountants, vehemently opposed it. The variable rate gave a sense of power to these accountants, who had people pleading with them for better rates.

'But don't you understand? A fixed price for the day would open up so much time for us to do our other work,' argued Gujarmal. 'A large part of our day is spent in arguing and haggling with people over rates,' he added. The munims were still not convinced. However, Gujarmal overrode all dissent and instituted a daily fixed price for his products. The other traders laughed and predicted a great financial loss for the Modis. But to their and the munims' surprise, not only did the business of Gujarmal go up, but he soon came to be seen as someone people could trust blindly. In less than a year, over 90 per cent of all orders came with the buyers sending their indent without even asking about the price as they were sure that the price would be the same for all.

# 4

## *The Turbulent Twenties*

THE decade of his twenties was a good one for Gujarmal when it came to his work. However, on a personal level, he was going through a bad phase. Even though he had been married in 1915 and was living with his wife since 1917, Gujarmal and Rajban Devi did not have a single living child. Rajban Devi had borne children almost every alternate year but no child had been able to survive for long after birth. Gujarmal was a deeply religious man and believed strongly that children, especially a son, were required to attain moksha. The Modi family, too, was an orthodox one when it came to these religious beliefs. Thus, the pressure on Gujarmal to have a son increased each year, and with each death of a newborn child, Gujarmal became more despondent.

It was not only the larger family that kept the pressure on Gujarmal, it was Gujarmal himself who believed that he must have a son. Till now he had not been faced with failure. Not being able to sire a son caused a deep sense of frustration in him as he saw it as a personal failure. The same parents who had always told him that he could achieve any goal he set his mind to were also the ones disappointed by the lack of a grandson. Though they couched it in gentler language, it was clear to Gujarmal that he was coming up short when it came to ensuring the continuation of the lineage. Gujarmal started having mood swings and even symptoms of mild depression. These gave rise to episodes of loud anger and irritation.

It was one of these bouts of anger that led to trouble with Maharaja Bhupinder Singh. Patiala in the 1920s was a rich riyasat, and Bhupinder Singh was known for his wild and extravagant lifestyle. The tales of his hedonism and his love for the good life—wine, women and song—are well known. The British indulged the maharaja and he reciprocated by providing them with generous hospitality. There were many British officers in the riyasat and the maharaja treated them all, even the junior ones, with much respect. The common people took their cues from the royalty and thus treated the Britishers with reverence. Some Britishers took advantage of their position and treated the local people with contempt. One such Britisher was a garage inspector called Turner. He was a particularly abrasive man who treated all Indians in an insulting manner. Though Gujarmal did not know Turner personally, he had heard about the Britisher's behaviour.

Public auctions were a regular part of Indian life in the early twentieth century. At one such public auction, Gujarmal and Turner were both present. The auction was being held in a large ground. The auctioneer had set up his table under a tree and the bidders, and many people who had come just to observe, were sitting on the ground. There were some chairs scattered as well.

The auctioneer held up Item Number 15. As he did so, a murmur went around the gathering. Item Number 15 was a silver inkpot and was of interest to many people. The auctioneer stated the bid price and then looked around for bidders.

'I am bidding for this,' a booming voice announced from the front row. Everyone craned their neck to look at the bidder. It was Turner who had announced his intention. As he spoke, he got up from his chair and looked around with his eyebrows furrowed. It was a message to everyone to refrain from counter-bidding.

A hushed murmur went around the group again. There were others who had been interested but now were having a rethink. Everyone was aware of Turner and his reputation. No one wanted to be at the receiving end of his insults. One or two men even got up, dusted their clothes and went to stand with the observers as if to convey to Turner their intention of not bidding. The others just waited for the hammer to go down so that the silver inkpot could be taken by Turner.

Before the auctioneer's hammer could come down, sealing Turner's bid, a loud voice bid a higher price than Turner's. A collective gasp went around the gathering as everyone was shocked that someone could take on the Englishman.

It was Gujarmal, who was sitting at the other end of the row of chairs. He looked at the auctioneer and repeated his bid.

The auctioneer, an Indian, looked at Gujarmal and raised an eyebrow as if to ask if Gujarmal wanted to take the risk. Gujarmal nodded.

It was not that Gujarmal was unaware of Turner's reputation. It was simply that Gujarmal did not think of Turner as anyone superior to him. To Gujarmal, Turner was just another Britisher enjoying the hospitality of the maharaja of Patiala.

Turner was surprised that someone had outbid him. As he looked towards the loud voice and saw that it was Gujarmal who had bid, Turner's temper rose. He was angry that an Indian was outbidding him. In a loud voice Turner raised his bid and continued to look at Gujarmal threateningly.

Gujarmal seemed oblivious of the hostility and calmly increased his bid again. This infuriated Turner and his face started going red. It had become a matter of prestige for him now. He had made it clear to all that the silver inkpot was to be his and to walk away from the auction without his prized item would be almost an insult for him. Turner was certain that his reputation would take a dent.

Turner increased his bid again. By now a couple of men had reached Gujarmal and were whispering in his ear. They were advising Gujarmal to stop the bidding as they feared the actions of Turner. But Gujarmal was not afraid. He had been brought up hearing his mother's lesson—'Son, do not be weak. Be strong. You are second to none.' He truly believed that he was equal to, if not superior to, Turner.

Gujarmal was aware that the bidding could go on for a long time. He was also aware that he could afford to spend more money than Turner could. He wanted to finish the bidding. His objective was not to prolong the process of bidding; he wanted to take the inkpot home.

Gujarmal's next counter-bid was thrice the amount that Turner had bid. The offer was way over the value of the inkpot. But the intangible value of the inkpot had suddenly become priceless.

Turner could not bid higher than Gujarmal. His face was red by now and he was barely holding back his temper. As the auctioneer's hammer went down in favour of Gujarmal, Turner got up from his chair and ran towards Gujarmal. The people who had gathered around Gujarmal took hasty steps back.

As he saw Turner rushing towards him, Gujarmal stood up. He was a tall man and had a bushy moustache, much like his grandfather had. And he was built like a wrestler. In his customary attire of a silk achkan and churidar, with polished jootis, and a vibrant safa on his head, Gujarmal was an imposing figure.

For a moment Turner stopped but then anger took over again. He tried to reach Gujarmal's collar but found that he was too short to do so. Totally frustrated, Turner started shouting. 'You bloody Indian! You native! How dare you? How dare you bid against me? Who do you think you are? Don't you know I am an Englishman? All you Indians are filthy, lowly creatures...' he ranted, almost frothing at the mouth.

A crowd had gathered around the two men by now. Keeping a healthy distance between themselves and the men, they watched the drama. A couple of onlookers hitched up their dhotis and squatted on the ground, prepared to sit for a while as the dramatic scene played out in front of them.

But the drama did not remain verbal. Gujarmal, who had been calm till Turner started shouting, lost his cool. The words used by Turner against Indians enraged him. He slapped Turner hard on the face. The Englishman fell to the ground with the impact of the slap. As he fell down, the people around took a collective step back with a gasp.

An Indian slapping a Britisher was not ordinary. Most of the men watching were actually delighted that Turner had been slapped. No one had liked what Turner had said. No one had liked how Turner used to behave. But they were also apprehensive about what would happen to Gujarmal. They waited with bated breath.

They did not have to wait long. Turner was aghast that an Indian had slapped him in front of other people. The fact that he had fallen was adding to the rage Turner was feeling. From the ground, he looked up and saw Gujarmal looming above him, standing with his arms folded across his chest.

Turner started getting up, dusting his clothes and shouting expletives at Gujarmal. Hearing curses about his mother and sisters, Gujarmal saw red. His emotions got the better of him. With one hand, he took Turner by the collar and started punching him with his other fist. All of Gujarmal's internal anger and irritation was manifested in this physical fight.

As he hit Turner again and again, Gujarmal kept shouting, 'You ask me who I am? How can you call all Indians filthy and lowly creatures? I will show you what a bloody Indian is!'

It took four men to control Gujarmal. They held on to Gujarmal to prevent him from hitting Turner, who, by now, had fallen back on the ground. No one wanted to go near Turner and they left him lying there by himself. Gujarmal was hustled away from the scene.

Within minutes, everyone in Patiala came to know about the fight. The local grapevine then worked almost as well as social media today. Gujarmal became an even bigger hero among the community for taking on a person like Turner. But the locals were worried about Gujarmal. '*Pata nahin bechare ko kya sazaa denge maharaja sahib* (Wonder what punishment the maharaja will give him),' said one in a hushed tone; '*Kaam to badiya kara hai Gujarmal ne, magar dekho ab kya hoga* (Gujarmal did a great thing, but let us watch what happens next),' said another.

People did not have to wait long. The news had reached the maharaja's court, and since an Englishman had been hit, Bhupinder Singh himself got involved. Gujarmal was asked to present himself in front of the maharaja.

'So, young man, what do you have to say about your behaviour?' thundered the maharaja. 'Did you hit Mr Turner?'

The maharaja was surprised that Gujarmal admitted immediately that he had hit Turner.

'But don't you know that he is an Englishman and the British are our rulers? Even the most common Englishman has to be treated with respect—I expect you to know this, Gujarmal,' said Bhupinder Singh.

'I know this, Maharaja Sahib,' replied Gujarmal. 'But I was angry because Turner had called you all kinds of names. If you are okay for an ordinary garage inspector to insult you, then I admit I am at fault.'

Now it was Bhupinder Singh's turn to be surprised. 'You mean he called me names, this Turner?' said the maharaja as he looked around at his courtiers perplexed, because no one had told him that Turner had insulted him. 'You say that he insulted *me*?'

Gujarmal looked steadily at Bhupinder Singh, smiled a little and said, 'Turner called all Indians bloody filthy, lowly natives. Are you not an Indian, Raja Sahib? Is insulting an Indian not insulting you?'

Bhupinder Singh had no answer but he understood what Gujarmal was saying. He could not punish Gujarmal now.

The matter was settled without any punishment meted out to Gujarmal. The local community, when they heard this news, erupted in joy and Gujarmal's reputation soared higher.

Bhupinder Singh was impressed with Gujarmal's fortitude. The maharaja had dealt with Multanimal for years and had come to respect his integrity over time. Bhupinder Singh realized that Gujarmal, like his father, was a man of integrity and character. However, some courtiers told him to be careful of Gujarmal, as the young man had the makings of a rebel. Bhupinder Singh ignored these warnings for now but they were going to come back to his mind later.

***

All through the 1920s, Gujarmal was waging an inner battle with himself over the failure of his marriage to produce a son. The couple had lost ten children and it took a toll on his wife. She grew weak and infirm. Gujarmal started brooding even more, feeling somewhat responsible for his wife's condition. He spoke to his father about the futility of a life without a son. He told Multanimal that he wanted to give up all worldly possessions and go to Rishikesh to live there to find the meaning of life. Multanimal could feel his son's agony but did not quite know what solution to offer as he, too, believed that a man must have a son to carry forward his heritage. Bearing a son was also seen as a sign of masculinity.

Multanimal could offer only one solution to his son—that of a second marriage. This suggestion was rejected outright by Gujarmal. 'How can I have another wife when I can barely take care of my first one?' said Gujarmal. 'There is no guarantee that I will have a son with a new wife. Why waste another girl's life?'

Everyone around Gujarmal could see that the young man was fast losing interest in work and even in living a life. Gujarmal was the eldest son of Multanimal and had a special place in his father's heart. Rukmini Devi was also concerned about Gujarmal. But she could offer no solace to her son. Instead, she suggested to Multanimal to try another route to reach Gujarmal. Rukmini Devi wanted Multanimal to call their daughter-in-law's father to come and talk to Gujarmal.

Multanimal finally called their daughter-in-law's father and briefed him about the situation. Together, the two fathers spoke with Gujarmal. With years of experience behind them, they were able to break through the mist in Gujarmal's mind. The young man agreed to get married again. His father-in-law was keen for his younger daughter to marry Gujarmal, but that proposal was refused by Gujarmal. However, once the news spread that Gujarmal was ready for marriage, proposals flowed into the Modi household. The family finally selected Dayawati, the daughter of Lala Cheddamal of Kasganj, and solemnized the marriage in June 1932.

The second marriage proved to be another turning point in Gujarmal's personal life. His passion for life and work returned and his despondency fled. Dayawati and he would have six daughters and five sons over the following years. Dayawati was to have a strong influence on Gujarmal's life going forward.

By the time Gujarmal married Dayawati, he had already expanded the family business in diverse areas. In 1928, he had purchased a cotton mill and an oil mill, combining them to create Modi Ginning and Oil Mills. In 1929, he had wanted to set up a vanaspati mill in Patiala but was not given permission to do so. When Gujarmal asked about the reason for refusal, he was not given any logical answer.

The reason that Gujarmal wanted to start manufacturing vanaspati ghee was based on the high demand for the product. The Dutch company Levers had made vanaspati ghee popular under the brand name of Dalda. People in India had traditionally used coconut oil, mustard oil and ghee for cooking and frying. But ghee was an expensive product and not everyone could afford it. The Dutch company had seen an opportunity in the market and started selling hydrogenated vegetable oil as a substitute for desi ghee. They even called Dalda vanaspati ghee. The concept caught on quickly as Dalda had the look and feel of ghee. The biggest advantage was, however, the price of Dalda, which was a fraction of desi ghee. Dalda had almost a monopoly in the Indian market. Gujarmal wanted to tap into this ever-growing market to manufacture and then sell vanaspati ghee. He was upset at the approval for a new manufacturing unit being withheld. That's when the first thoughts of moving out of the riyasat germinated in his mind.

The thoughts of leaving Patiala were kept in abeyance as there were other matters that needed his attention. His uncle, Girdharilal Modi, requested him to help him set up a new cotton mill in Nabha, a place not too far from Patiala. Even though he was a young man, Gujarmal was seen by everyone in the family as the go-to man for any new ideas and for the setting up of any new factory. None of his brothers or cousins had been able to earn the same respect within the family. Gujarmal viewed each opportunity to do something new as a learning opportunity. Thus, he was willing and eager to set up the new factory even though it was hard work and he would be away from home. After helping his uncle, Gujarmal also helped set up the Chamber of Commerce and Industry in Patiala. This was a big step in the Patiala region as the chamber brought together diverse businessmen to discuss matters of common interest. A well-known economist and former auditor general of India, Sir Frederick Gauntlet, was invited to inaugurate the Chamber of Commerce and Industry. The inauguration gave Sir Frederick an opportunity to meet and interact with Gujarmal. The Englishman was impressed with the business vision articulated by Gujarmal. Sir Frederick advised Gujarmal to think big when it came to business and to look beyond Patiala.

This advice of the Englishman resonated with Gujarmal as he, too, had been thinking about expanding the scope of his business and establishing factories outside the riyasat. But he was held back by his father. Multanimal did not want Gujarmal to move out of Patiala. Besides the fact that he was fond of his son, Multanimal also knew that Gujarmal was the one who was handling the business. The father knew that none of his other sons could manage the affairs as well as Gujarmal. Thus, every time Gujarmal voiced his ambitions, Multanimal would stonewall it, many times using emotional blackmail. But with each passing year the desire to move out of Patiala and set up large businesses grew sharper in Gujarmal. The administrative environment in Patiala was also not giving any comfort to Gujarmal's plans of expansion. The Patiala administrators had already refused permission for a new vanaspati factory and Gujarmal was facing a similar issue once again.

It was 1931 when Gujarmal came upon an opportunity to buy a flour mill in Ludhiana. He saw it as a chance to start his expansion outside Patiala. However, Multanimal put his foot down and refused to give permission for Gujarmal to leave

Patiala. 'But, Father, I am getting constrained in Patiala. You saw that I was not given permission for the vanaspati factory,' said Gujarmal. Multanimal was adamant. But Gujarmal was not one to give up easily. He persisted and a compromise was reached between father and son.

'You can set up any factory anywhere in the world, son,' said Multanimal. 'But promise me that you will reside only in Patiala and not set up another house anywhere else.' Gujarmal gave his word to his father and went off to Ludhiana to supervise the work on the flour mill. An engineer was employed for the restructuring of the mill and over a hundred workers were contracted. The work on the flour mill was proceeding well when the family loyalist, munim Gopal Shah, brought the news that Multanimal was not in good health and wanted Gujarmal to come back immediately.

Gujarmal rushed back to Patiala and found that it was not an emergency after all. He was upset with his father for having called him under false pretences.

'Father, you seem to be better now. I will return to Ludhiana as the factory there needs my supervision,' said Gujarmal.

Multanimal, however, had other ideas. 'Ever since you have gone to Ludhiana the work in Patiala has suffered. I am not involved in the day-to-day work, but I do hear from people that it is slipping,' he said.

'But, Father, you have not been involved in the day-to-day work for many years now,' argued Gujarmal politely. 'And the work is continuing well under the supervision of our munim ji. And I do come back every week to oversee things here. You know this.'

But Multanimal would have none of it. Though he had given permission to Gujarmal to set up factories outside Patiala, Multanimal really did not want his son to leave him. The father was aware of the ambitions of his eldest son and knew that once Gujarmal tasted the blood of freedom, it would be difficult to contain him. Gujarmal, chafing under the constraints placed by his father, had to rein in his ambitions once again because he could not, and would not, go against the wishes of his father. It was the family culture that the word of the father was the law.

Having failed to win the battle with his father over the mill in Ludhiana, Gujarmal had no option but to shelve his plans. The money spent so far was wasted. Nevertheless, Gujarmal shifted his focus back to Patiala and submitted an application to the administration to set up a cloth mill. The application was approved and Gujarmal started work on the levelling of the site to set up the mill. The workers in Ludhiana were given an option to move to Patiala to work on the construction of the new factory. Gujarmal also organized capital, a sum of ₹15 lakh—not a small amount in 1931. The plans were progressing well but the administration, suddenly and without any explanation, cancelled its earlier permission. No amount of requests and petitioning to the maharaja would get the administration to change its decision of cancelling the permission for the mill.

Gujarmal was very angry but could do nothing as it was the maharaja of Patiala who had given the order. The maharaja may have had a reason to withhold his permission for a new mill in Patiala as British India was going through political unrest at that time. Mahatma Gandhi had already started his non-cooperation movement, and the country had seen a number of strikes and tool-down days at various factories. It is speculated that the maharaja was wary of new labour coming into his riyasat. The new cloth mill would have required at least two to three thousand workers, which could have led to disturbance, given the volatile situation in the country. However, Gujarmal was not aware of any of this and knew only that permission was once again refused to him. First the vanaspati factory and now the cloth mill. His determination to move against the arbitrary rulings and whims and fancies of the maharaja became stronger. But the question remained: how was he going to convince his father?

***

It was at this time that fate played a role in Gujarmal's life once again. In 1932, there was a party at the Patiala palace. The maharaja had won a court case against one of his contemporaries and was in a mood to celebrate. The parties of the maharaja were well known for their decadence. Wine, women and song were accompanied by rich food. Though Gujarmal did not enjoy the ostentatious display of wealth, he could not refuse the invitation. He was also not comfortable seeing money being spent on hedonistic activities. Having grown up in a wealthy household himself, Gujarmal believed that the owners of wealth were merely the custodians of it for future generations. Even though fairly well off, the Modi house was austere. The entire Modi family were staunch vegetarians and teetotallers.

Gujarmal decided that he would go to the party at the palace for a short while. He could not miss the bhajan session at home that same evening and decided he would wish the maharaja and rush back home.

When he reached the palace, he found it lit up with bright lights. People in their finest clothes had gathered and were enjoying the hospitality of the maharaja. The mood was wild and swinging. Alcohol was flowing like water. Gujarmal was offered a glass of wine but he refused.

As the evening wore on, the noise and the revelry increased. Gujarmal's acquaintances and even complete strangers kept coming up to him and asking him why he did not have a glass in hand. Gujarmal politely kept refusing all invitations to drink. He was waiting to meet the maharaja so that he could wish him and then go home.

The maharaja was in an inner room with some of his close associates. As he walked out towards the larger gathering, people started going to bow down to him and wish him. A couple of men went up to Bhupinder Singh and whispered in his ear.

'Sahib, there is something wrong with Gujarmal. It seems he is not happy at your victory,' one said in a low voice.

'Why do you say this?' asked the maharaja.

'He has refused to have a drink all evening. We have asked him ourselves, but he keeps declining,' said the other man.

Bhupinder Singh was a tad upset. To a Punjabi, a glass of alcohol is not just a glass of alcohol. It is a symbol of friendship. Refusing alcohol is inferred as refusing friendship. However, the maharaja was not prepared to believe other people. He beckoned Gujarmal.

Gujarmal had been waiting all evening to meet the maharaja. When he saw Bhupinder Singh calling him, he rushed to him. Before he could congratulate the maharaja and then beg leave, the maharaja spoke.

'What is this I hear, Gujarmal? You are not happy that I won?' asked Bhupinder Singh.

'Why do you think I am not happy, Your Highness?' countered Gujarmal, quite perplexed.

'People are telling me that you refused to have a glass of wine. Come on. You cannot refuse me. Here, have a glass of wine and we will toast my success together,' said the maharaja jovially and gestured to an attendant to bring a glass of wine.

'Sahib, I do not drink alcohol at all,' said Gujarmal in a quiet voice while declining the server. 'It is not that I am not happy for your victory, but I have been taught never to touch a drop of alcohol.'

The people who were gathered around the two, and were watching the proceedings with great interest, started talking to each other in hushed tones. 'How can anyone refuse an instruction of the maharaja?' asked one man of the other. 'Gujarmal has made a mistake. He should have taken at least one sip. After all, the maharaja himself had offered it to him,' said another. 'Isn't it an insult to the maharaja?' wondered yet another man. Unaffected by this, Gujarmal bowed low, congratulated the maharaja on his victory and then requested the maharaja to excuse him.

The party ended late that night but the matter of Gujarmal refusing to accept a drink from the maharaja started creating more noise. People close to the maharaja insinuated that by refusing wine Gujarmal was casting aspersions on the lifestyle of the maharaja himself. Others went further to say that there may have been a larger conspiracy behind Gujarmal refusing a direct order. Still others reminded Bhupinder Singh of the time when Gujarmal had beaten the Englishman Turner. The maharaja remembered that incident clearly and also recalled that he had been told by his courtiers to watch out for the young man as he had all the traits of a revolutionary. Surrounded by people who kept implying insubordination by Gujarmal, the maharaja had to take some action. He issued an order banishing Gujarmal from his riyasat.

The maharajas in British India did not have powers to imprison anyone without a proper court hearing; but they could exile people. The rulers of principalities could, in effect, banish people so that the exiled persons had to, perforce, leave the riyasat.

Gujarmal was humiliated by this banishment. He was a proud man with firm convictions. He had been brought up in a household where alcohol did not form part of the lifestyle. But he did not believe that his lifestyle was in any way inferior to one with alcohol. It was true that Gujarmal was not quite comfortable with the manner in which the maharaja lived his life. Extravagance of any kind was seen by Gujarmal as unnecessary. The only place where extravagance was acceptable to him was when it came to work.

Though Gujarmal had been wanting to leave home to expand the businesses, he did not want to leave home under a cloud of being banished. The humiliation slowly turned to anger. He knew that he could not fight the maharaja in any battle or war. But he decided that he would fight the maharaja in another manner. At the back of his mind an audacious plan started forming—a plan of setting up a township of his own. A township which would not be based on an extravagant lifestyle but on a lifestyle rooted in hard work. A township where people would follow the rules and laws. A township that would run on the principle of equality and where people would live with dignity. A township where he could be the equivalent of the maharaja!

As Gujarmal thought more about a township, the anger was replaced by a bubbling excitement. The humiliation that he continued to feel was pushed to the back of his mind. Gujarmal focused on the life ahead and stopped looking at the life gone by. He was also happy that his father could not stop him this time. After all, it was a dictate from the maharaja and Multanimal could not overlook it.

Gujarmal's simple refusal of a glass of wine in Patiala set off a chain of events that would ultimately result in a township named after him.

# 5

# *How to Build an Industrial Township from Scratch*

EVER since his run-ins with the administrative arbitrariness of the Patiala regime, Gujarmal had been chafing against it. He also was fed up of watching the decadent lifestyle of the royal family and their courtiers. He had been taught by his mother since childhood that any wealth earned should not be used for an ostentatious lifestyle. The royal family's overt hedonistic lifestyle clashed with his own values. Gujarmal had grown up to believe that wealthy people needed to undertake stewardship. He also believed that wealth generated had to be employed for the benefit of people and that the owners of the assets were mere trustees.

With all this in mind, Gujarmal looked forward to his exile from Patiala with great excitement. He was thirty years old and brimming with plans for setting up new factories and mills outside the constricting environment of Patiala. He wanted to set up not only mills and factories but also housing facilities for the workers. In his mind he saw a township that revolved around the establishments set up by him; he saw the township as a planned space with an ample number of green parks, educational institutes and temples. He wanted his workers and their families to live happily in the township. The various restrictions in the Patiala riyasat rankled deep within and he was sure that his township would be a model one.

He shared his dream with his father. Multanimal was struck by the expanse of his son's dream. Even though he knew that Gujarmal had to leave Patiala due to the order of the maharaja, he was convinced that after a time he could request Bhupinder Singh to revoke the order. Multanimal wanted his son to come back, live with him and manage the family business. Thus, he was conflicted. He felt proud of his son and his determination, but he also did not want Gujarmal to do so well outside Patiala that returning home would no longer be an option.

'Your dream to set up an industrial township is commendable, son,' said Multanimal, 'but where are you going to get the money for it? I hope you know that I am not going to give you any money to set up a new township.' In his heart, Multanimal hoped that the lack of financing would be a damper for the bright ambitions of his son.

'I know, father,' replied Gujarmal. 'But I do not want your money. I only want your blessings and good wishes. They mean more to me than all the money that you could give me.' Saying so, he folded his hands and bowed his head in front of his father.

'Son, you cannot live your life only by emotions,' said Multanimal as he patted his son on the head and raised it so that he could look at Gujarmal. 'You will need money to set up your township. Who will give you the money?' asked Multanimal as he looked into his son's eyes, again hoping that Gujarmal would revise his plans.

'Father, no one will *give* me any money,' said Gujarmal brusquely, as if irritated at the thought that he would need to ask for charity. 'I will have to sell my concept to the investors so that they will willingly invest in my business. I am convinced that I will find investors for my industrial township,' he added in an explanatory tone.

Gujarmal was correct when he said that good ideas and good businesses had no dearth of investors. The business and investing environments under the British rule were very different from the ones after 1947. The stock markets had been in existence since the late 1800s but there were many other opportunities for investors as well. These opportunities were presented by the managing agency system.

The managing agency system had, in fact, evolved in the second quarter of the nineteenth century in India. The system was adopted by London as an efficient way to manage joint stock companies operating in the Indian subcontinent, especially where the shareholders of the companies had no first-hand knowledge of the business. The system worked as follows: the managing agency operated essentially as an entrepreneur. When the managing agency saw a business opportunity, for example, a cotton mill, it raised venture capital from friends and associates of the managing agent or promoter. The shortfall in funding, if any, was borrowed from a bank. With the funds in hand, the managing agency bought the mill and set it up to operate. Once the mill and the business were running successfully, the managing agency sold its majority shareholding to the public and it became a listed company. However, the managing agency signed a long-term management contract with the company, which gave it the right to continue to manage the business. The profits earned by the managing agency became capital that could be invested in some other business, say, a flour mill. The managing agency, despite its small shareholding, continued to manage the cotton mill and the business thereof due to the long-term management contract with the mill business. Typically, a managing agency made key decisions on behalf of its operating companies, which included the products to manufacture, the markets to target and where to get the raw materials from. The advantage of the managing agency system was that it enabled the agency to control and run a number of business enterprises with a small financial stake in each. A managing agency's ability to raise capital from the bank and the public depended on the promoter's track record and reputation.

Gujarmal, even at the young age of thirty, had earned a reputation for his business acumen and integrity. The factories in Patiala were testament to his ability to manage the day-to-day execution of the business. Thus, he was convinced that the investors would buy into his concept of an industrial township.

While he had no doubt about potential investors and their interest in his business plans, he was not so sure about his wife. It had been only six months since his marriage to Dayawati. He spoke with her gingerly about his plans.

'Of course you must follow your dream,' Dayawati replied with enthusiasm. 'I may not be able to accompany you in the beginning but be sure that I will be praying for your success every moment.'

Dayawati, then, and in the years to follow, was the source of his strength and inspiration. A traditional Hindu girl, Dayawati was gentle, compassionate and literally worshipped and adored her husband. She was a young girl, not yet twenty years of age, and was uninformed about the details of the business. At her in-laws' house, Dayawati spent her time taking care of Gujarmal's family. Since she spent a large part of her time with her mother-in-law, Dayawati's values of worldly and business matters were moulded by Rukmini Devi. The young bride, too, learned the concept of karma yoga and the benefits of a simple life. She was ready to support her husband in every way she could and therefore encouraged Gujarmal to follow his dream without worrying about her.

Gujarmal was relieved and asked her if she wanted to go to her parents' house when he left. Dayawati was only too happy to go and spend more time with her parents. So Gujarmal left his wife at his in-laws' house and set forth to fulfil his dream.

***

Gujarmal left his home with ₹300 in his pocket. His destination was Delhi, which was directly under British rule. Gujarmal believed that the business environment under British rule would be less arbitrary. However, he still did not have a clear idea about how to begin his new life. Reaching Delhi, he checked into a hotel and paid upfront for a month. He began consultations with some business acquaintances and started visiting the markets to better understand the opportunities. As he spent time with the traders and merchants, Gujarmal heard everyone talk of Calcutta as the hub of trade in India.

Calcutta, indeed, was an important commercial hub of the Indian subcontinent. The city had been developed by the British

East India Company and then by the British Empire. Calcutta had been the capital of the British Indian Empire till 1911. It was one of the largest ports in Asia and, once established, the entire northern India became a hinterland for the Calcutta port. The inland customs duties had been abolished in 1835, creating an open-market system, and the railways had begun their construction in 1854 to connect the city with other parts of India. The development of the railway network was one of the main factors for the quick growth of industry in Calcutta. The city had become a hub for British mercantile, banking and insurance companies. People from all over the country came to Calcutta to set up businesses and it became the busy hub of commerce in India.

Since he had not finalized any plans in Delhi for new business, Gujarmal decided to take a trip to Calcutta to explore opportunities there. After his first visit to the city, when he had gone to Calcutta to demand payment from Sahu, the fraudulent trader, Gujarmal had kept in touch with a few friends he had made there. This time when he visited them again, he stayed with Seth Narayan Das Bajoria—a reputed businessman of the city. Seth Bajoria introduced Gujarmal to others in the business community. Soon Gujarmal was in discussions with them to explore new opportunities. They had the knowledge of the commodities in demand in Calcutta, a major port. As he spoke with traders, Gujarmal heard them all talk of vanaspati ghee, which was in great demand in India. The name—vanaspati ghee—was a misnomer as the product was not ghee in the technical sense; it was hydrogenated vegetable oil that mimicked the look and feel of ghee. Dalda was the only branded product available nationally and was doing great business. The product used to be imported, largely from Holland. Gujarmal had previously tried to set up a vanaspati ghee factory in Patiala but had not been given permission. He now decided that he would set up a vanaspati ghee factory in Calcutta and started scouting for land around town.

However, he had to give up his plan to produce vanaspati ghee once again. This time it was due to a change in the excise duty on sugar. The British government had increased the import duty on sugar in late 1932 as they wanted to promote its domestic manufacture. Suddenly there was a surge of interest among Indian manufacturers as sugar was a product that was always in high demand. Gujarmal saw the increase in the import duty as a sign from God for him to drop his vanaspati plans and to focus on setting up a sugar mill instead. Calcutta and the area around it were not ideal for a sugar mill, however, and thus Gujarmal headed back to Delhi.

As he started working on a plan for a sugar mill, Gujarmal knew that he had to get the funding for his mill finalized as the first step. It was only when he had the money in hand that he could start looking for the land. As a starting point, he looked towards his extended family.

His uncle and cousins were successful and wealthy businessmen in Hapur, a city close to Delhi. Gujarmal had helped his uncle and nephew set up their factories in Hapur a couple of years earlier and had spent time with them. While in Hapur, he had interacted with his uncle's friends and acquaintances who were mostly traders and mill owners. As a result, when he went to Hapur in 1932, the local business community was already aware of his resourcefulness. There Gujarmal shared his idea of an industrial township, and the sugar mill as the first step towards it, with his uncle and cousins. They liked the idea of the industrial township and encouraged Gujarmal to follow his dream.

Gujarmal set up his company under the managing agency scheme and called it Modi Sugar Mills Ltd. He requested his uncles to organize a meeting with the other wealthy investors in Hapur. At that meeting, Gujarmal made an impassionate presentation about his idea of a township where everyone would have a job and the families would have a good environment to live in.

'I plan to have many green parks where the ladies and elders can take their walks and children can play. I plan to have schools and colleges so that the children of the workers can get the best education. I also plan to have temples and gurudwaras so that people can worship their God,' he proclaimed in the meeting.

'But where will this township be located?' asked one businessman.

'Have you found a place yet?' asked another.

'I know what I want in the location and I have no doubt that I will finalize it soon,' replied Gujarmal. 'But I cannot even begin to start negotiations with the landowners till I have the funds. Therefore, I have set up the company and am selling shares to interested people.'

A good business managed well under a managing agency system generated great returns for the investors. In the modern-day stock market, seasoned investors look at the business model as well as the promoters and management. Even in 1932, seasoned investors made their investment decisions after they had assessed the promoters and the managers. The investors were aware of Gujarmal already. Now they asked him questions about the plan for the mill and the details of the business. They looked at the plan shared by Gujarmal and looked into the person who would manage the business—again Gujarmal. His past work and reputation, along with the convincing presentation, allowed the investors to decide. Within no time, shares worth ₹10 lakh were sold. The investors had to pay 50 per cent upfront for their shares. Thus Gujarmal, very soon, had a cash balance of ₹5 lakh in his bank.

With the funding secured, the next step for Gujarmal was to look for the right location for his sugar mill, and in turn, his township. The first item on his list, naturally, was the availability of a large area that could be developed into a township. The next was the availability of drinking water. Transportation links—including those of the rail and the road networks—were also important, as was the presence of a postal office. Gujarmal also wanted a police thana around the area as he wanted law and order to be maintained. He also wanted an area where the availability of labour would not be a problem. And, as he was beginning his township journey with a sugar mill, he wanted the township to be in an area that had fertile soil conducive to sugarcane crops.

With all the items on his list, he knew that it was not going to be easy for him to find just the right location. He requested for the loan of a car from his uncle to enable him to travel around Delhi and Hapur to scout for locations. He started his journey armed with a diary to scribble notes, a folding chair, a durrie (cotton rug), a warm blanket and some food items. He needed all these items as he was not sure that he would be able to return to Hapur each night. He drove every day looking for that ideal location but had no success. Sometimes there would be water and fertile soil but no rail or road networks; other times it would be an area that checked all the items on the list but the land was not available.

Undeterred, Gujarmal persevered. He could not go back to his father or even his uncles and other shareholders admitting defeat. The zeal to prove himself drove him day and night to look for the ideal spot. He had led an easy life in Patiala. His father was a wealthy man and the Modi household had all the comforts of that era. Gujarmal used to drive a Rolls Royce car in Patiala. He had left all that to follow his dream. He was not prepared to give it up so easily.

Many times, life rewards you unexpectedly. You may have been chasing success for a long time but without any luck and then one day, success comes and sits by you seemingly without any effort. The same happened with Gujarmal. As he was driving from Meerut towards Ghaziabad, he needed to stop for a bio break. The car stopped at a village called Begumabad.

Gujarmal went to relieve himself and as he started going back to the car, he decided to take a short walk to stretch his legs. As he walked and looked around, he could not believe his eyes. The area was just what he had been looking for! True, the area was a wild forest and had prickly trees and bushes, but it was well connected to the highway and he could see a railway track in the distance. The Ganga Canal, which provided water, was not far from Begumabad. He quickened his pace and walked faster—from north to south and then from east to west. The more he saw, the more he was convinced that his search had ended. Gujarmal was delighted that he had finally located a site for his township.

His uncles in Hapur, instead of being delighted, were apprehensive about the location selected by Gujarmal. He was told that the area was full of potholes that had snakes, that there were robbers around and even that it was haunted by ghosts. Even though Gujarmal was deeply religious, he did not believe in ghosts. He had seen the area and had spent the day walking around and was convinced that it was indeed the right spot for him. He also believed in his intuition, which was telling him that his decision was right. He told his uncles that to prove them wrong he would spend a night in that area in the open. 'We will see if there are any ghosts or robbers or snakes there,' said Gujarmal.

He did not need to spend a night in the open to convince his uncles but he did spend more days exploring the area. The village Begumabad was approximately 50 kilometres from Delhi, 32 kilometres from Ghaziabad and 25 kilometres from Meerut. It was situated on the national highway that connected these cities. The railway station was not far from the village. With each visit to the area, Gujarmal's resolve became stronger.

Gujarmal may have decided on the location of his industrial township but he still had to convince the landowners to sell him their land. Not only was the ownership of the identified area fragmented, but there were also land pieces that had multiple joint owners within the same family. It was a daunting task but Gujarmal was unfazed. Since he had identified the area for his township, he wanted to stay in the vicinity to facilitate the land purchase. He needed to rent a house for himself. As he asked around for a suitable house, he heard about one that was owned by the brother of the honorary magistrate of the area. The landlord stayed in one part of the house and was looking to rent out the other section. Gujarmal's interest quickened as he realized the value of knowing the brother of the honorary magistrate. He asked to be shown the house and readily agreed on the rent without haggling. This snappy thinking proved providential as Gujarmal built a rapport with his landlord after moving in. He also got introduced to the landlord's brother—the honorary magistrate, who was able to explain the intricacies of land purchase to Gujarmal.

Armed with his newly acquired knowledge, Gujarmal started two activities simultaneously. The first was to identify local munshis or brokers who worked on land transactions on a commission basis. For each plot of land sold, the munshi earned a handsome commission. Simultaneously, Gujarmal started meeting the landowners himself.

Gujarmal's morning started with a brisk walk for an hour and then physical exercises. After a bath, his puja and breakfast, he was ready for the long day ahead. He had a list of the landowners already and each morning he decided the ones he would meet that day.

It was fortunate that the summer and monsoon were behind him. The task of being out in the open would have been even more arduous in the hot summer. Thankful for the moderate weather, Gujarmal would drive as far as it was possible. Besides the main highway, there were not too many internal roads in the area. Gujarmal kept a bicycle in the car. Once he reached as far as the car could go, he would stop the car, take out his bicycle and start riding out.

The days may have been moderate, but the area was dusty. The strong breeze, though pleasant, swirled up dust all around. Gujarmal, mindful of the dust, wore a dark achkan and avoided white churidars. He still wore the vibrant safa on his head. He wanted to present a picture of confidence and good bearing when he met the landowners. Gujarmal presented an imposing figure as he rode his bicycle confidently, dressed in formal clothes.

Word had gotten around that a young man from Patiala was buying land in the area. As he would ride up to a landowner's house, Gujarmal could see the men sitting outside on charpoys, almost as if waiting for him. Getting down from the bicycle, with folded hands and head bowed he would greet the men. From the corner of his eye, he could see the women, with pallus over their heads, peeking from behind the door or window. Everyone was curious about the six-foot-tall young man who had the bearings of a wrestler but was a businessman.

Gujarmal would sit with the men and start to tell them about himself and the vision for an industrial township in the area. His message to the villagers was simple. He explained that his plan of setting up various factories and mills in the area would result in various avenues of employment for the locals. He took them through his plans of having pucca housing for all workers, gardens and parks for the residents, and schools, colleges and temples for the families of the workers.

Agriculture was not a high income generator for most farmers even in British India. With smaller landholdings, the agricultural produce was barely able to sustain most farmers. The villagers liked what they heard but were also apprehensive about selling their land. The village elders had often lamented the lack of industrial activities in the areas around Begumabad. They had seen other villages in more industrialized areas reap the benefits once the factories were set up. The younger lot was sceptical as their land was the only asset they had. Gujarmal talked to both the elders and the youth and, over a period of time, the villagers bought into Gujarmal's vision. Slowly, but steadily, the land deals started happening and before long, Gujarmal was the owner of 100 bighas, approximately 40 acres, of land. The registry process was duly carried out with the help of his landlord's brother.

Even as the land purchase and registry process was going on, Gujarmal had started working on the plans for the sugar mill and submitted them for approval to the local authorities. The approval process was simple and not tedious. The British government encouraged the setting up of industries. The buying of the land required permission but after that, there were no licences given out by the government to set up industries. Further, there was no price control nor a limit on production capacities. Gujarmal had already bought the land, and once the factory plans were approved, the sugar mill could be set up.

The next step for Gujarmal was to get the area cleaned and then levelled before the construction of the mill and other structures could begin. Sourcing the workers was no problem as Gujarmal got them all from the neighbouring villages and put them to work. After the plans were approved by the authorities, Gujarmal ordered the plant machinery from England. He was sure that by the time the machinery was delivered, the mill would be ready. He also set up a brick kiln to ensure regular supply of building material for construction.

While there were very few restrictions for the businesses under British rule, transportation logistics was the main obstacle. The road network was developed between the bigger cities but the hinterland had few tarred roads. Thus, transporting material was one of the biggest hindrances faced by Gujarmal. Setting up a brick kiln was one of the ways he could ensure proper supply of the building material.

The entire area was busy with activity. The smoke from the brick kiln kept billowing up to the sky looking down on the activity on the ground. If someone had seen the area from a height, the ground would have looked like an active ant colony, men and women scurrying around seemingly in no particular order. In reality, however, each worker belonged to a team that was led by a supervisor. Gujarmal had had experience of working with a large number of workers when he had set up mills and factories in Patiala. All that knowledge was coming in handy for the young man now.

Finally, the area was cleared of most vegetation. The next task was to get the ground levelled and the plinth of the factory determined. The actual construction could not start before that.

The plinth, though not talked about much, is an important part of the building. It is the part of the building above the ground up to the ground floor. An average person may see the plinth as keeping the creepy-crawlies out—a high plinth prevents crawling creatures and snakes from entering the building. However, there are other reasons for its importance from a construction point of view. When it rains, the surface water flows over the topsoil before it percolates to the softer parts of the ground. If the water flows at sub-floor levels, under the building, the structure can actually sink, leading the walls to crack. The plinth is the part of the building that provides stability to the building, and the hard soil-and-stone filling inside the plinth provides a stable structure for the floor.

Gujarmal had not spent the previous monsoons in the area and therefore did not know the flow of water. But he did know the importance of the plinth as every future structure would use the same measurement. He solved the problem of the plinth level by looking at the railway line. He was sure that the railway tracks would have been laid after a careful study by the railway engineers and that they would have taken the topography of the area into account. He used the level of the rail tracks as the marker and gave orders to start the construction accordingly.

The building came up under the supervision of Gujarmal. He stayed in the same house but spent almost sixteen hours out of it. Having overseen the construction of mills in Patiala, Gujarmal knew the art of engaging with the workers with friendliness on the one hand and discipline on the other. It seemed to him that within no time at all the plastering process for the sugar mill had started.

The mill was an imposing structure in the middle of an area that used to be only wilderness. The building rose up four storeys. One chimney rose high and went up 100 feet into the sky. The mill had big windows that drew in the light. The roof was sloping and dotted with skylights that helped to bring even more light into the mill. People from villages around the area came just to stand in awe of the building coming up. Gujarmal was happy with the interest his mill was getting and hoped that it would be ready before the nine-month deadline.

But nature had other plans and Gujarmal had his baptism not by fire, but by rain. The monsoons arrived just when the plastering was almost complete. The entire mill got flooded. Gujarmal was perplexed as he had taken great care to follow the plinth level of the railway track. He worried about having got the measurements all wrong. He also worried about losing face in front of his workers. He worried about his reputation being tarnished. It was well known that he had taken great care in setting the level of the plinth. In fact, people had called him fastidious and some had even laughed at him then. One rain had brought all his efforts crashing down. Not only was the mill flooded but the house he was constructing for himself was also damaged. As he stood in knee-deep water, frowning at the sight of his entire mill flooded, totally distraught, a worker came running to him, splashing the water all around.

'Sir, the water is being stopped at Sikri. Some villagers have built a bund (a small kuchha mud dam) to prevent the water from flowing through. That's why all this water is getting accumulated here,' said the worker in a rush.

The villagers of Sikri were upset over the upcoming mill as those who earlier worked in the fields of the big farmers had started working at the construction site. These workers were being paid better rates and did not want to go back to farm labour. The rich landowners of Sikri saw the Modi mill as a threat and wanted to stop it before it started. The rain came as a heaven-sent opportunity for them. The village was at a slightly lower level than the Modi mill area and, as a result, whenever it rained, the water flowed from the mill area through Sikri village and further down, where it turned into a rivulet. The villagers knew that if they put up an obstruction and did not allow the water to flow down, the mill area would get flooded.

This is exactly what happened. A small bund was built in no time at all and the water found that it could not flow through. As it continued raining and the water started accumulating, the entire mill area got flooded. The rich landowners of Sikri believed that the mill would be severely damaged by the water and Gujarmal would have no choice but to abandon the project.

Gujarmal was both relieved and angry. He was relieved that the measurements for his mill were correct and that the problem of flooding was man-made. However, he was angry at the villagers of Sikri. A simple man-made mud bund had threatened to undo the work of a year. The bund endangered the very vision of the township that Gujarmal had. The sugar mill was to be the starting point of the township, and Gujarmal was seething with anger that a group of villagers had given themselves the power to come between him and his dream.

By now, if there was one lesson Gujarmal had learnt, it was to keep his anger in check. He asked the worker to accompany him to Sikri village. He spoke to the village elders there and requested them to break the bund to allow the flow of water. The villagers saw Gujarmal's request as a sign of weakness. Instead of agreeing, they increased the security at the bund by placing a watchman there.

Gujarmal faced a dilemma. If he engaged in open confrontation with the villagers, it would harm him in the long run. If, on the other hand, he did not take any action, not only would his reputation as an able businessman get tarnished, but his dream would not even take off. As he sat quietly contemplating his next set of actions, he remembered what his mother had always told him—'Son, don't be weak. Be strong. But be fair.'

An idea started developing in his mind and the more he thought about it, the more he liked it. Once he finalized it, he decided to act on it. Gujarmal took only a couple of his people into confidence for this plan. He developed his strategy based on the knowledge that the area around Begumabad was infested with robbers belonging to the Maria tribe. Such was the fear of these robbers, who did not hesitate to beat up their victims, that no villager liked to venture out after dark. Gujarmal took advantage of this. He went over the plan in detail with his two compatriots—Ravi and Subhash—and waited for nightfall. It involved the use of a gun.

Gujarmal had a revolver and he planned to use it.

***

The rain clouds started appearing again as the evening light started falling. Gujarmal was happy at this development. He needed a dark night for his plan to work. In spite of the dark clouds, there was no rain. Instead, there was a strong wind and a storm threatened to break soon.

The three men—Gujarmal, Ravi and Subhash—had worn dark clothes so that they would blend into the night. Gujarmal had the pistol in the pocket of his kurta. The area was in darkness as the moon was behind the clouds. The villagers and the workers had all retired for the night. The group of three moved silently towards the bund. As they reached it, they ducked behind some bushes and waited for the watchman. They did not have to wait long. A small point of light became visible in the distance. It was the watchman patrolling the bund, smoking a beedi.

The three men waited patiently behind the bushes. They saw the watchman come closer to the end of the bund. Before turning back to resume his patrolling, the watchman stood for a moment, took a deep puff of his beedi and threw it into the bushes. The beedi missed Ravi by a few inches and he flinched. Gujarmal held on to Ravi and gestured for him to be absolutely quiet.

The watchman turned his back and retraced his steps as he patrolled the bund. Once the watchman had moved a few yards away, Gujarmal began to execute his plan.

Two things happened simultaneously. Ravi got up and ran towards the guard, keeping to the undergrowth. He made sure that he made a loud noise as he crashed through the bushes. As the guard stopped, hearing the noise, Gujarmal fired in the air a couple of times. The sound of the shots being fired was loud and clear. As he heard the shots, Ravi stomped around even more loudly and started shouting at the top of his voice. '*Bachao, bachao! Mujhe maar daala!*' (Help me, they have killed me) wailed Ravi full-throatedly as he continued to loudly crash through the undergrowth.

The guard, who had been trying to find the source of the noise, turned motionless at the sound of the firing. And then, as he heard Ravi shouting for help, ran full speed but in the opposite direction. The guard was sure that it was a bunch of the dreaded Maria robbers and he did not want to be near any of the members of that tribe.

As soon as the guard ran for safety and left the bund unattended, Gujarmal, Ravi and Subhash got to work. They broke through the mud dam to create various channels for the water to flow through. Within minutes, they saw the water gushing through the channels they had created. Their work for the night over, the three men walked silently back to the mill area. By the time the three men reached the sugar mill, the water level inside the building had already receded. Gujarmal swore Ravi and Subhash to secrecy once again and the three men went their separate ways.

The next morning brought in the news that the villagers of Sikri were livid at their bund being broken. Everyone on the construction site was surprised and wondered how the bund had broken. Gujarmal, secretly smiling within, told his workers that he would go and speak to the villagers again. He went to Sikri village and offered cash assistance to the villagers to build a proper channel for water to flow from the sugar mill area through their village. He also offered to buy their land at attractive prices. The villagers had no proof that Gujarmal was responsible for the breach in the bund. The offer of cash was attractive. Gujarmal himself had a friendly but forceful personality, and he used all the charm he could muster. The villagers knew they had been beaten at their own game and thought it best to take the offer being made by Gujarmal.

***

In less than a day, the mill area was back to being a beehive of activity. Though the workers had no proof of it, they were sure that their boss—Gujarmal—was responsible for the quick solution. Stories of robbers and people being shot had already started gaining momentum on the local grapevine. Gujarmal was sure that the story was started by the watchman, and with each telling it gained more colour. The workers felt energized as they felt that had won the match. And so Gujarmal did nothing to stop the exchange of the stories of fierce robbers and the brave watchman.

By now the news of the upcoming sugar mill had reached Patiala. Multanimal was both surprised and delighted at the news. Even though he had full faith in his eldest son, Multanimal was still taken aback that Gujarmal had been able to gather finance, buy the land and construct the factory this quickly. Overjoyed, he decided to pay his son a visit.

Gujarmal welcomed his father and took him around the site, showing the work with great pride. As Multanimal went around, he realized that the sugar mill was going to be successful and profitable. The shrewd-businessman instincts in him along with pride for his son made Multanimal proclaim to everyone at the mill that he was buying shares worth ₹2 lakh in Modi Sugar Mills Ltd. Gujarmal was happy as his capital went up by 20 per cent immediately and he increased the installed capacity from 600 to 800 tonnes.

The work at Begumabad continued at a hectic pace. Meanwhile, Dayawati and Gujarmal were awaiting the birth of their first child. Dayawati had come to Begumabad once the work on the factory started. Since Begumabad was virtually a village, the medical facilities left a lot to be desired. Gujarmal, having lost many children already, was very concerned about the first pregnancy of his second wife. He decided to send her to Patiala as not only were the medical facilities better, Gujarmal's parents and extended family were there to look after her.

One day, just a few weeks before the factory was to be completed, Gujarmal got news that Dayawati was seriously unwell. The pregnancy was creating some serious health issues. He managed to speak with the doctor and the prognosis was not very good. Gujarmal, having suffered the loss of children, was worried. He dropped everything and rushed to Patiala.

As he entered the family house in Patiala, he saw his father sitting in the verandah. Multanimal was surprised to see his son as Gujarmal had sent no prior information about his arrival.

'What are you doing here, son?' asked Multanimal as Gujarmal bent down to touch his father's feet.

'I heard that Dayawati is unwell. I was concerned and so I rushed here,' replied Gujarmal while looking around. 'Where is she? How is she? Is she okay? Is the baby okay?' asked Gujarmal in a rush.

Multanimal leaned back into the chair and looked at his son with searching eyes. 'Are you God?' he asked his son.

Gujarmal looked perplexed at his father, not understanding the question.

'Do you not trust us with the health of your wife, son? Do you think we are not taking care of her?' Multanimal continued.

Gujarmal was at a loss for words. 'Wh ... why would you think so, father?' he spluttered. 'Of course I trust you and everyone here. Why wouldn't you take care of my wife?'

'So, if you think that we are capable of taking care of her, why have you left everything and rushed back here?' asked Multanimal. 'You know that the investors have put in a lot of money for the new factory. Even I have invested money. Should you not be focused on that, son? There are people here who can take care of your wife in your absence. But who is taking care of the building of the factory while you are here?'

Gujarmal understood what his father was conveying to him. He realized that he had the responsibility of ensuring the investors' interest. It was a huge responsibility.

'We are all here, son, and will let you know if you are needed. But keep faith in God and all will be well,' said Multanimal. 'Now go back and ensure that the factory comes up on time.'

Gujarmal left immediately, without even meeting his wife. He carried with him a lesson that he would never, ever forget—work was his first priority and the investors who trusted Gujarmal with their money had to come before his own family.

When he got news of the birth of his daughter and that Dayawati was in good health, he was relieved. The new father was happy but wished that a boy had been born. The earlier doubts and sense of failure for not having produced a son were tucked far back into his mind but had not been eliminated. But he could not spend much time worrying about the lack of a son as his sugar mill was nearing completion.

Modi Sugar Mills was inaugurated on 15 September 1933, almost a year after Gujarmal had left his father's house. It was a record of sorts that in a year Gujarmal had identified the land, procured the funding, purchased the land, ordered the machinery and got the mill constructed. As one person after another came up to Gujarmal to congratulate him, the young man's mind saw the sugar mill as just the first step in his quest to set up an industrial township.

# 6

# *The Start of an Industrial Empire*

MODI Sugar Mills was ready for business in the middle of September 1933. However, the sugarcane-crushing season began only in end-October–mid-November. Gujarmal did not want the mill and the workers to remain idle for two months. He had got the mill up and running and had the workers on the payroll. He did not want the workers to get used to receiving their wages without doing any work. So he decided to start manufacturing sugar using the desi khaand (jaggery powder) and gur (jaggery). Besides testing out the machinery and the refining process, and keeping his workforce gainfully employed, Gujarmal also wanted to test the new foreign experts he had hired.

While the sugar mill was still under construction, Gujarmal had started scouting for talented chemists and panmen. A panman is an expert who supervises the entire process of sugar production. From operating the vacuum pans to boiling the syrup to ensuring that the exhaust or live steam valve is opened at the right time to let the pan's hot steam boil the syrup; from monitoring the temperature and pressure gauges to maintaining the correct boiling pressure to finally cleaning the pan with steam—the panman has to supervise all the delicate processes. A chemist is an absolute necessity in a sugar mill, because the refinement, essentially, is a chemical process.

To his surprise, Gujarmal had found that there was no local talent available. After the government had announced an increase on the import duty for sugar, many opportunistic businessmen had seen this as an occasion to set up sugar mills. As a result, more than thirty sugar mills had come up in the country in less than two years and it had become difficult to recruit talented technical people as most were already employed. Instead of being frustrated at the lack of availability of local talent, or settling for second best, Gujarmal enlarged the scope of his search for talent beyond India. Soon he had a Dutch chemist and two panmen from Java at the sugar mill. But these foreign recruits had not come cheap. Gujarmal had to pay high salaries and sign a legal contract with the foreign experts. They also demanded a fully furnished house, two full-time servants and two months at a hill resort during the summer. Europe was in a recession and the employment opportunities there were not robust and these demands from the foreigners were outrageous. But Gujarmal had no choice but to accede to the experts' wishes as he wanted the best for his sugar mill.

On 31 October, a month and a half after the inauguration of the sugar mill, 35,000 mann (1 mann = 40 kilograms) of khaand was delivered at the factory. This was melted and then processed to produce refined sugar. Gujarmal was delighted that the machinery and processes worked and therefore ignored the loss that he made on the operation. As a raw material, khaand was more expensive than crushed sugarcane juice would have been. But Gujarmal did not care as his mill was fully operational.

The sugarcane harvesting season began in early November 1933 and Modi Sugar Mills was working to capacity. The first season of any business is a pilot phase—all systems and processes along with man and machinery are tested under live conditions. Modi Sugar Mill, its people and its processes were also tested.

Gujarmal found that while the machinery was working fine, it was the people who were giving him trouble. He also found that the output of sugar was much less than what he had calculated. Gujarmal took a deeper look into the working of the mill. He did not like what he found.

The Dutch chemist was one of the main reasons for the people problem. The Dutchman was lackadaisical in his approach towards the work. It could have been because he was a white man and thought that he was above the 'natives', or it could have been that he was not used to the hard work that was the norm at all Modi factories. His behaviour had a ripple effect on the other workers. They, too, began taking shortcuts in their work and taking days off without informing the foreman. Gujarmal also found that due to a lack of supervision, a large amount of processed sugar was being left in the pan and was being washed out with water once the pan was cleaned. Sugar was literally being thrown down the drain.

Gujarmal knew he could fire some people, including the Dutch chemist. But he also knew that he could not let the Dutch chemist go because the sugar mill needed an experienced chemist. At dinner time he discussed the matter with Dayawati.

Dayawati had taken charge of the Modi house in Begumabad. She had used the year spent at her parents' house to study some more. Gujarmal had discovered that, even though untrained in business, Dayawati had a sharp mind. She could grasp the nuances of any situation quickly and was unafraid to give her opinion when asked. What had delighted Gujarmal the most, however, was that Dayawati took a keen interest in learning the game of bridge. This card game is considered to be a cerebral game. It combines logic and reasoning with science, maths and problem-solving. Gujarmal had taught his wife the game of bridge and each evening they played together. He had come to realize the value of Dayawati's logic and advice.

When she heard about the problems at the sugar mill, Dayawati thought for a moment. She then looked at Gujarmal and suggested an alternate plan. 'Firing someone is easy. But it does not solve the problem, does it? It will create more problems for you because you will not have a chemist in the factory,' she said. Gujarmal nodded as he listened to her. 'So, why don't you instead set a better example for everyone to follow. Even that Dutch fellow will have to follow,' she continued.

'What are you suggesting?' asked Gujarmal.

'Move into the factory for two weeks. Stay in the factory. Don't come back home. Let the workers see that you are there every moment of the day,' she suggested.

Gujarmal laughed out loud. 'My own wife is throwing me out of my own house!' he said and looked up, as if appealing to the gods. But he saw merit in Dayawati's suggestion. 'I could move my bed into the office,' he thought aloud. 'And I could eat with the workers,' he continued.

'No, no, no!' said Dayawati immediately. 'I will send you food every day. Hot breakfast just the way you like it and then lunch and then dinner. You may just need to get the tea made at the mill itself,' she added. 'This way you will be able to observe everyone at all times and, most importantly, they will see that you are observing them.'

Gujarmal mulled over the idea and liked it. He liked the fact that he would get to see the problem first-hand instead of relying on some reports presented by his people.

The workers were surprised to see the owner move into the factory. His office was realigned to accommodate a bed. Gujarmal started supervising the supervisors and also started interacting with the workers. It took two weeks but after that, there was a visible difference in the energy of the people and their engagement level with their work. The output of sugar went up as well. After two weeks, when he was confident that the workers had all got out of their bad habits, he went back home.

It is unusual for a new sugar mill to make profits in the first season of operation, but Modi Sugar Mills bucked the trend. Though small, Gujarmal made a profit at the end of the first season. He may have been the only one among the other sugar mills in the area to do so, but when it came to the matter of mill labour, he too was facing the same problem as the others were.

***

All the workers in the various mills and factories in Begumabad had transitioned from farm labour to their new jobs. The rich zamindars saw their workforce grow smaller and smaller. The zamindars tried to hold on to their farm labour but the workers were not interested. For one, the factories paid more, and two, the workers did not have to work outdoors in the scorching sun or in the harsh winter cold. The zamindars were powerful people and some of them got together and started petitioning against the mills. Gujarmal took the lead in starting a conversation with the zamindars. He explained to them that the mills actually helped the rich landowners.

'How can you say this, Gujarmal ji?' asked one old landowner as he sat on the charpoy, drawing on his hookah. 'Your factory is taking away all our labour. How can we benefit from this?' The other zamindars nodded in agreement.

'Don't you know that the price of land has already gone up?' counter-questioned Gujarmal. 'If I want to buy the same land as I did last year, I will have to pay substantially more.' Gujarmal explained that with the area getting industrialized, not only would the land value continue to go up but there would be better road connections to the national highways as well.

As they listened, some of the zamindars nodded for Gujarmal's talk resonated with them. But the others were still not convinced.

'That is all right, prices may go up, but who will work on our land?' asked a portly zamindar as he took a sip of hot tea.

'You need people to work in your mills and we also need workers on the farm,' added another zamindar with a large bushy beard.

Gujarmal heard them and understood the problem they were faced with. 'The solution is to get more people to come from outside our area and start working here,' he said. 'My plan is to create a township and it will not only be my workers who will stay there. As the area develops, it will attract more people from near and far. Together we will provide employment opportunities for outsiders—you in your farms and I in my mills,' he added.

As he saw most of the zamindars nodding, he continued with his logic. 'How many times have we wished that this kuccha road would become better? With the mills running, the government will have no choice but to create a pucca road—a tarred road. You will also be able to take your produce to the market faster and easier.' His narrative went on to include the establishment of educational institutes to take care of the workers' children. 'Your children and grandchildren will also be able to avail of the good education opportunities then,' promised Gujarmal.

Gujarmal conducted these series of meetings with different groups of zamindars. He used the time after the first crushing season for this outreach. It was slow but the tide of opposition started turning. Before the new year began, the resistance of the zamindars had watered down.

***

After Gujarmal had left Patiala in 1932, Multanimal's business had started flagging. Though he had his other sons helping him, not one of them displayed Gujarmal's acumen. Multanimal wanted Gujarmal to shut down the sugar mill and come back to Patiala. He had spoken with the maharaja and had got the exile dictate revoked. However, Gujarmal was adamant that he would continue on his path to create an industrial township. He still had not got over the humiliation of having been exiled. Besides, his deep desire to set up his own township was still burning strong.

Gujarmal was sure that he wanted his own township—a fiefdom of sorts; a town where he would treat all people with dignity and work towards the benefit of those living there. Gujarmal had been disenchanted by the opulent display of the hedonistic life led by the royals of Patiala. He was also not comfortable with a rule by the whims and arbitrary fancies of the ruler. As a resident of the riyasat, he had felt the pain of not being the primary concern of the royals. In his own township he wanted the average resident to believe that the township and the leaders were there to make the lives of the residents trouble-free. Therefore, he was unwilling to give up on his dream and told his father so.

Back in Begumabad, Gujarmal started the preparations for the second season of the sugar mill. His dream of establishing a flourishing township had started taking shape. Once the sugar mill was ready, Gujarmal started the construction of housing complexes for the workers and their families. These were pucca houses, owned by the company and rented out at nominal rates to the workers. Areas had also been earmarked for parks, and the planting of flowering shrubs and leafy trees had started. Gujarmal also wanted to establish a school as soon as he could because he wanted the workers' children to have access to good education. Dayawati supervised the construction of the temples in the area. Coming from a traditional household, she was a deeply religious lady. Gujarmal and she had continued the practice of having a daily bhajan session at their home.

Gujarmal had already started feeling a sense of ownership over the small settlement that had been developed and its residents therein. The workers and their families looked upon Gujarmal as their benefactor. As part of his morning walk, Gujarmal had started to walk along the railway line, from one end of the settlement to the other. Each day, as he looked around during his walk, he could not help but feel a sense of pride. 'This is my town, these are my people, and it is my duty to make their lives comfortable,' were the overriding thoughts in his mind each day. The mission he had set out to achieve had passed its first hurdle. It was a matter of time before the vision was fully achieved—such was Gujarmal's firm belief.

The sugarcane season of 1934 came along with its many problems. Some were man-made while the others were a result of nature playing truant. It had been a long tradition among Indian farmers to use sugarcane to produce gur. Even in 1934, over 55 per cent of all sugarcane produced was used to make gur. In earlier years, the farmers had no option but to do so. This was because refined sugar was largely imported and there were no sugar mills to produce refined sugar domestically. But now that there were more than thirty sugar mills, and newer ones were being set up, the farmers actually had the option of selling their produce to the mills to make refined sugar. But it was difficult to get rid of old and entrenched habits. And so the farmers continued indigenously making gur.

The farmer could not be blamed entirely for wanting to use his sugarcane crop to produce khaand and gur. These could be produced either by the farmer himself or at facilities close to him. The cut sugarcane did not have to be transported to make gur. In contrast, it was not easy for the farmer to take the harvested sugarcane to the sugar mills. He needed to load up the bullock carts (there were almost no tractors or small trucks available to farmers in 1934) and then take them to the mills. The road network in the area was not developed and the kuccha roads were littered with potholes. The mills, on the other hand, could not operate without the harvested sugarcane.

This problem could not be solved in one year alone. However, Gujarmal started the work of petitioning the government to focus some of their attention on the road network to ease the flow of agricultural produce. It would take time, but the problem did get resolved in later years.

In 1934, besides the road network issue, Gujarmal ran into another obstacle. Some of the workers in his mill belonged to a lower caste, then referred to as harijans. In the entrenched Indian caste system, harijans were considered untouchables. Some of Gujarmal's compatriots were not comfortable that the upper-caste workers in the mill were intermingling with harijans. Pressure was put on Gujarmal to sack the harijan workers from the mill. Though Gujarmal was deeply religious and went to the mandir every day, he did not believe in the caste system. For him a worker that was diligent, honest and productive was the one that was important. In his own hierarchy, such a worker was higher than a lazy, non-productive worker of a higher caste. He, therefore, pooh-poohed the suggestion and, in fact, offered cash incentives and housing at reduced rents to some harijan workers to get them to work in the mill. No doubt these actions endeared him to the harijans, but many of the other mill owners were not happy about it.

The year 1934 was a test for Gujarmal. Besides the above man-made problems, nature added her own set of troubles in the year. The monsoons failed and the sugarcane crop was affected. The area around Begumabad that was used to grow sugarcane was also an area that was affected by the failed monsoon. As a result, Modi Sugar Mills had to get sugarcane from far-off areas like Hardoi, Shahjahanpur and Bareilly. This increased the cost of the raw ingredients, and the second year was not a good one for Modi Sugar Mills.

It had not been a good year for Multanimal's business in Patiala either. Lack of proper supervision and guidance had resulted in losses in the factories. Even the business of supplying rations and other items to the army was in the red. The commissions from the managing agency system were good but these were being used to offset the losses in the other businesses. Multanimal was feeling the absence of his eldest son. He sent word to his son in Begumabad to drop everything, shut down Modi Sugar Mills and take over the business in Patiala again.

The previous year, Gujarmal had refused to move to Patiala. After the second season, in early 1935, he refused again. He told his father that he was now responsible not only for himself but for the thousand other workers and their families. 'I am not even talking of our shareholders, father. People who trusted me and invested their money in my company. I have spent the last two years setting up a mill, housing complexes, and you should see the gardens—they are coming along very well too. I have many people now dependent on the mill. It will be extremely difficult for me to put all of them in jeopardy,' continued Gujarmal. He decided, however, that once the mill was running smoothly, Gujarmal would spend more time in Patiala.

***

The third season of sugarcane crushing brought joy for Dayawati and Gujarmal as they were blessed with another daughter. Vimlakumari was born in May 1935. Gujarmal was still unhappy at the lack of a son but was grateful that he at least had two children.

After two years of Modi Sugar Mills, he was still haunted by the failed crop of 1934. Fortunately, the sugarcane crop in 1935 was fine and the sugar mill was working full steam ahead. But a new problem raised its head that year. The productivity of the sugar mill was much below the standard. No matter how much Gujarmal tried, the production did not increase.

Once again, Gujarmal turned to dreams. Earlier in his life, he had followed what he had seen in his night-time visions. Looking at it from another point of view: he believed in sleeping over his problems to find a solution.

He applied this to sort out the issue of the mill's falling productivity. Before sleeping, he would meditate and focus on the matter bothering him. One night as he slept after meditation, Gujarmal had a dream in which he saw a mahatma—an old seer. The mahatma was an old man with a flowing white beard. He seemed to know the problem Gujarmal was facing. The old seer told Gujarmal to add milk of lime to the sugarcane juice to see results. After saying this, the mahatma disappeared.

Gujarmal awoke with a start. Even though it was very early, Gujarmal woke up feeling absolutely fresh and with a clear mind. He immediately called for the Dutch chemist and told him to add milk of lime to sugarcane juice as part of the refining process. Milk of lime is calcium hydroxide suspended in water.

The Dutch chemist was aghast at the instructions he received. 'Milk of lime? In the sugarcane juice? Why, sir? How can I do this? The juice will be spoilt,' he asked in quick succession. And then he laughed. 'Oh, I see, you are joking, sir!' said the Dutch chemist with a broad smile. 'But you could have chosen a better time. I was sleeping when I was called to meet you.'

Gujarmal looked at the Dutch chemist calmly and said, 'If you think it is a joke, then let it be. I will ask your assistant.'

The Dutch chemist did not know if his boss was playing a trick on him. But he had not heard of anyone adding milk of lime to sugarcane juice. He waited as Gujarmal called for

Desraj Narula, who worked under the Dutch chemist. Narula was given the same instructions. Unlike the Dutch chemist, who had questioned Gujarmal, Narula simply folded his hands and said, 'As you say, Modi Sahib.'

The next day as Desraj Narula went about adding milk of lime in the refining process, Gujarmal went about settling the dues of the Dutch chemist. Gujarmal had not liked the manner in which his chemist had made fun of his instructions. Even though he had no idea whether or not the addition of milk of lime would increase productivity, Gujarmal did not want to have men around him who mocked him. The Dutch chemist was sent packing the same day.

The news of Gujarmal's dream spread fast throughout the worker community. The workers, too, were eagerly waiting for the results of following the instructions their boss had received in a dream. After his day at the factory, Gujarmal went home. Desraj Narula and the workers remained and worked late as they wanted to see the outcome.

It was midnight and Gujarmal was woken up by a loud knocking on the main door of his home. Ensuring that Dayawati and their daughters were not disturbed, Gujarmal quickly put a chadder around his shoulders and went to the door. An excited Desraj stood there, hopping from one foot to the other. As soon as the door opened and Gujarmal stepped out, Desraj bent to touch the feet of his boss.

'Modi Sahib, you are great,' cried Desraj. 'It worked! We produced over a thousand boris of sugar today, sahib!'

Gujarmal was surprised and happy at the same time. 'A thousand boris! That is great. Did we not produce four hundred boris a day till now?' he asked Desraj, who nodded vigorously. Adding milk of lime to the sugarcane juice had worked.

The productivity of the mill increased by over 150 per cent. Gujarmal's worries about the third season being a washout were over.

Later, Gujarmal asked the local laboratories to analyse the scientific reason for the increased productivity. It was found that sugarcane juice, kept for a period of time, became sour and acidic. This resulted in the sucrose content in the juice converting into molasses, which made the liquid less sweet. The milk of lime prevented the sucrose from changing. Thus the amount of sugar that could be produced from the same amount of liquid went up significantly. Today, adding calcium hydroxide to sugarcane juice is an integral part of the process for pH correction. However, in the 1930s, it was a new scientific discovery.

# 7

# *The Ways of Bureaucracy*

AFTER the completion of a successful third season, Gujarmal decided to take a break and take his family to Kashmir. On the way, the family stopped in Patiala. Once at the family home, Gujarmal got word that the maharaja wanted to meet him. The maharaja had already revoked the exile order but Gujarmal's sense of humiliation had not gone away. One part of his mind told him to stay away as the maharaja had insulted him by banishing him from Patiala. The other part of his mind, however, encouraged him to go for the meeting as, this time, he could speak about his own township. In a small way, he was the ruler of his little fiefdom.

The news of the success of Modi Sugar Mills and the fledgling township had already reached the ears of the maharaja. Gujarmal was met warmly in court. As the two men spoke, Gujarmal felt the small but definite change in the manner he was being treated. However, he was still surprised when the maharaja asked if Gujarmal could help him in a matter. Bhupinder Singh said that it was a delicate matter and he believed that Gujarmal would be the right person to help him. His surprise changed to intrigue; Gujarmal found himself agreeing without even knowing the problem.

The maharaja explained that a well-known industrialist of the area, Hari Krishna Lal, owed a large amount of money to the riyasat. Hari Krishna was a resident of Bhatinda and had many factories in different places in the riyasat. He had borrowed large amounts of money from various banks against the security of his factories and land. State Bank of Patiala had also loaned Hari Krishna a large sum against the surety of one of his factories. Hari Krishna's account had turned into a non-performing asset—NPA—as he was unable and unwilling to pay neither the interest nor the capital borrowed. The maharaja's chief minister as well as the finance minister had tried to get Hari Krishna to pay up but had failed. Since it was the State Bank of Patiala, it was an embarrassing matter for the maharaja. He was apprehensive that if Hari Krishna was allowed to get away without any consequences, other borrowers may also stop paying back their loans. It was to recover this money for the riyasat that the maharaja requested Gujarmal's help.

Gujarmal heard the whole matter, thought for a minute or two and then said, 'Maharaja Sahib, I will handle this. Don't worry.' The maharaja immediately offered the services of a hundred armed guards who could be of help to Gujarmal.

'What will I do with these people armed with weapons? I don't need them,' said Gujarmal.

The maharaja was surprised and asked again, 'Are you sure you don't want any police guards, Gujarmal? How will you get him to pay you if you don't have armed people with you?'

'Do not worry, Maharaja Sahib,' replied Gujarmal calmly. 'Please give me a few weeks. You will have your money.'

Even though the maharaja was sceptical, he had no option other than to wait a few weeks.

Gujarmal went home and told his family that he would not be able to accompany them to Kashmir. Instead, he went off to Bhatinda. One of the reasons that it had been difficult for the bank and the maharaja to get back the borrowed sum from Hari Krishna was the fact that the Bhatinda factory was managed by a Britisher—one of the many political agents of the British government who had control over major activities. It was difficult, even for the maharaja, to go against the British political agent, who wielded tremendous power and influence in public life. No one could dare to even enter the factory without the permission of the Britisher. But Gujarmal had no plans of entering the factory. His plan was completely different.

Once in Bhatinda, Gujarmal invited the British manager and his secretary, Tara Chand, to have tea with him at the guest house. Gujarmal's reputation had spread in the Patiala riyasat and the British manager was curious to meet this person who was establishing an industrial township after being banished from the riyasat.

The Britisher and Tara Chand were welcomed warmly by Gujarmal and a couple of his confidants. A lavish tea was spread out for the two visitors. However, Gujarmal refused to have anything except water as he said that he had an upset stomach. As Gujarmal was telling the British manager about how he acquired the land for the sugar mill in Begumabad, he suddenly clutched his stomach and winced. 'I have an upset stomach. I need to excuse myself for a bit,' he said apologetically to the British manager. 'But please enjoy the tea and snacks. I will be back shortly.' He nodded to his confidants as he left the room. They nodded back as they knew the role they had to play in the ongoing drama.

Gujarmal rushed out of the guesthouse from the back door and went straight to Hari Krishna's factory. The people in the factory knew that their British manager and secretary had gone to meet Gujarmal. Further, Gujarmal had an imposing personality. Dressed formally in silk clothes with polished shoes and the customary vibrant safa on his head, Gujarmal had a personality that could not be overlooked. As he walked in confidently and with complete authority, the office people welcomed him into their chambers. Once there, he demanded the keys to the cash box. In the 1930s, the monetary assets of a business were not kept in the bank, as the transactions were not as simple as they are now. Thus, most businesses kept almost all their money in the cash box or a safe. Anyone who had control of the safe, and therefore the money, in effect had control of the factory.

The cashier, looking at the confident well-built, tall man in front of him, was overawed by his personality and did not suspect any foul play. Thinking that the Britisher wanted the keys and had sent Gujarmal to get them, he handed over the keys willingly. Gujarmal then asked for the duplicate set of keys and was told that the British manager did not trust anyone and therefore had only one set of keys for the safe. Once Gujarmal was sure that he had total control of the safe, he went back to the guest house.

The British manager and Tara Chand had been enjoying themselves and had not realized that Gujarmal had been away for some time. The confidants knew and upon his return, by a gesture of his hand and a nod of his head, Gujarmal conveyed to them that he had been successful. As per their plan, soon after Gujarmal's return, the confidants and others left the room, leaving Gujarmal alone with the British manager and Tara Chand. Once alone with the two men, Gujarmal told them what had been accomplished during the time they were enjoying the tea and snacks.

The British manager and Tara Chand were horrified. Their faces lost colour as they were both ashamed and afraid. The manager and his secretary knew that they would become a laughing stock and objects of ridicule once the story of how easily Gujarmal was able to dupe them became public. Additionally, they were frightened of the wrath of the maharaja. With the keys to the safe, the maharaja owned the factory and could punish them for their earlier disregard of the riyasat. Besides these emotions, both of them also saw a financial loss for themselves as they were sure to lose their jobs and, given the manner of their ousting, it would be difficult for them to find another job easily.

Gujarmal knew all this and offered both of them a deal. He told them that both of them could keep their jobs provided they signed some papers. The British manager looked at Tara Chand and nodded. Both men agreed. As his mission was accomplished, Gujarmal returned to Patiala.

The maharaja could not believe that Gujarmal had been successful in such a short time and without any altercation. To reward Gujarmal, the maharaja appointed him the official receiver for the retrieved factory. The official receiver was a prestigious post and a coveted one as the appointed person was responsible for the liquidation of the property. The post of official receiver carried not only prestige but also financial rewards because the officer was paid for his duties.

The maharaja believed that his troubles were over once Gujarmal took control of the factory. He had not accounted for the anger of Hari Krishna Lal. When the industrialist heard about the fracas at his factory, he was livid. Hari Krishna complained to the British government that the maharaja had taken over his factory by cheating and fraud. In 1935, the relationship of the maharaja with the British Viceroy in India was strained and the two were not on the best of terms. Gujarmal was sent for again, this time urgently, by the maharaja as he feared that the Viceroy may take some action against him.

Gujarmal met the maharaja again and heard what had happened. 'Don't worry, Maharaja Sahib,' said Gujarmal calmly. '*Main hoon na* (I am here) and no harm will come to you.' Even though unsure as to how Gujarmal would handle the matter, the maharaja had no choice but to leave it to the young man.

Once the inquiry was started by the British government, a charge of taking over the factory by force and stealth was levied against Gujarmal and the maharaja. Gujarmal denied this charge vehemently. 'I have not done any fraud. You are questioning me and my character—and I resent it strongly,' asserted Gujarmal in his booming voice.

The opposing party continued to maintain that the British manager had been cheated.

'Have you asked the British manager and Tara Chand?' asked Gujarmal confidently.

'We don't need to ask anyone anything,' replied Hari Krishna, brusquely cutting off Gujarmal. 'You have cheated me and I want my factory back.'

Gujarmal took a moment to survey the small room and the people within. He then asked his attendant to hand him some papers from the bag he was carrying. Taking hold of the papers, Gujarmal went through each of them. Then he handed over the papers to the court officers.

The officers almost snatched the documents from Gujarmal and started going through them. As they did, they realized there could be no case against the maharaja and Gujarmal.

The officers were looking at the documents that Gujarmal had made the Britisher and Tara Chand sign at the guest house. When Gujarmal had gone to Bhatinda, he had already carried the legal transfer deeds of the factory with him. These transfer deeds were signed by the Britisher and Tara Chand. Since these were signed and sealed documents, the British government had no case against the maharaja. He was acquitted of all charges.

The maharaja was beside himself with joy. He had been apprehensive about the case. He realized that he could trust Gujarmal completely and started consulting him on other matters of state. Gujarmal's work in Bhatinda earned him brownie points with the maharaja and some life lessons. One key lesson was insight on the workings of bureaucrats.

***

The Bhatinda factory was running well under the British manager, who was now supervised by Gujarmal. However, there was still some amount outstanding from the loan taken earlier from the State Bank of Patiala. Gujarmal's plan to recover that amount included auctioning some land that was part of the assets of the factory but was not used by them. Accordingly, he issued a public notice of the auction, giving the details of the land. Unknown to Gujarmal, the deputy commissioner of the area had had his eyes on that tract of land for a while. Upon seeing the public notice, the deputy commissioner sought a private meeting with Gujarmal. After the pleasantries, the bureaucrat came straight to the point. He suggested that Gujarmal cancel the auction and instead sell the land to him at below market price. He also said that he would share the amount thus saved with Gujarmal.

Gujarmal was aghast that such a proposition was being made to him. 'I am beholden to the maharaja,' replied Gujarmal calmly. 'He has made me official receiver even though I am not even a high-school pass. I will never do anything to harm the interest of the maharaja.' Though he spoke coolly, he was seething within as it hurt his sensibilities that people thought he could be corrupted.

Gujarmal, to a large extent, was a self-made man. Leaving behind the wealth and business of his father, he had started from scratch in Begumabad. The past few years had brought him success, which he knew was the result of his hard work and focus. He also believed that he could achieve anything once he set his mind to it. In all of this, Gujarmal neglected to factor in the importance of the ancillary people around him. Bureaucrats were one set of such ancillary people. Gujarmal thought that the bureaucrats were rightly called 'babus' as they showed lack of entrepreneurship and followed the rulebook. He failed to acknowledge their importance in the business world. He was to now learn his lesson.

Gujarmal thought that the matter had ended with the deputy commissioner. Indeed, it had for Gujarmal. But the deputy commissioner felt insulted. A deputy commissioner in the government was a big officer in the early twentieth century and wielded great power over the public. The big and powerful government servants were used to obsequious behaviour by people around them. Even a suggestion from these bureaucrats was taken as an instruction by other people. The deputy commissioner was angry that Gujarmal had dared to disregard his suggestion. He waited for an opportunity to pay Gujarmal back.

The opportunity presented itself not long after. It happened when the revenue minister of the riyasat went to meet the deputy commissioner in the latter's office. Since it was hot weather, the rooms were cooled by placing slabs of ice in front of a fan. The deputy commissioner knew that Gujarmal was visiting Bhatinda and was in the factory. He sent his clerk to the factory with a note to Gujarmal asking for a slab of ice. However, he sent no money for the ice. Nevertheless, Gujarmal himself paid for the ice, entered it in the sales register, cut a challan or gate pass and then sent the ice to the deputy commissioner. When the clerk went back with the slab of ice, the deputy commissioner asked him if he had paid for it. 'No, sir, Modi Sahib did not ask for money. He gave it to me for free,' replied the clerk. The gate pass issued for the ice slab also showed the ice being sent without charge. The deputy commissioner filed the gate pass in his personal file and this incident in his memory bank.

Yet another opportunity came the way of the deputy commissioner some time later. Gujarmal had planned to travel to Bhatinda and had bought a train ticket accordingly. On the day of the travel, Multanimal decided to accompany his son. So, another ticket was bought for his father. The problem was that Gujarmal had bought a first-class ticket while Multanimal travelled only in second class. Thus, even though he had a ticket for the first-class compartment, Gujarmal had to sit with his father in the second-class compartment. As fate would have it, the deputy commissioner was also travelling in the same train to Bhatinda. He was surprised to see Gujarmal travelling second class because he knew that the official receiver was allowed, by the maharaja, to travel first class. He managed to take a photograph of Gujarmal and his father in the second-class compartment.

Soon after this, the deputy commissioner lodged a formal complaint with the maharaja. He charged Gujarmal for giving away ice slabs of the factory for free, causing the factory and the maharaja financial loss. He also accused Gujarmal of charging the maharaja for first-class travel but travelling second class and keeping the balance fare for himself. The photograph of Gujarmal in the second-class compartment and the gate pass for the 'free' ice slab was attached with the complaint. The maharaja immediately called for a court hearing and summoned Gujarmal.

When Gujarmal heard about the charges, he was upset. He was further upset that the maharaja had believed the charges. He called for the sales register and showed the entry where he had paid for the ice slab. He further produced the train ticket bought for first class and explained to the court the reason for him travelling second class. The case was dropped but it left a bitter taste in Gujarmal's mouth. He realized that bureaucrats could not be trusted and that he had to be wary of them going forward. The maharaja, however, wanted to make up for this incident and offered Gujarmal the contract to run the factory in Bhatinda at a discounted rate.

Gujarmal had had his fill of Bhatinda and wanted to have nothing more to do with the city or the factory. He let his cousin Harnam Modi take the contract and kept himself away from there. He had much more work to do in Begumabad.

# 8

# *Expanding the Modi Business Empire*

BACK in Begumabad, Gujarmal and Modi Sugar Mills prepared for the fourth season of sugarcane crushing. The first three seasons had been individually eventful. The first had seen a small profit while the second had seen a loss. The third season had seen the increased productivity of sugar due to the addition of milk of lime in the sugarcane juice. This increased productivity had, in fact, led to a problem now being faced by sugar mill owners in 1936.

Sugar production had increased by over 60 per cent in less than three years, ever since the government had increased the import duty on sugar. The other mill owners had started following Gujarmal's example of adding milk of lime. As a result, the productivity of all sugar mills had gone up. Further, the number of mills had also gone up to over 130. The supply of sugar in the market by 1936 had become far more than the demand for the product. Thus, the prices of sugar started falling. Gujarmal did not want a year of losses. He had more plans for his industrial township, and he could not execute them if the first factory he established kept running into losses.

As was usual with him, he slept over the problem of falling demand leading to falling prices. When he woke up the next day, the solution was clear in his mind. He called for a meeting of the sugar mill owners and suggested that they form a syndicate. A syndicate is a temporary alliance of businesses that work together for a common objective. In this sugar syndicate, all mill owners agreed to sell only after agreeing on the prices together. It was not illegal in 1936 to form a cartel to sell products. There was no price control by the British government nor any penalty for any restrictive trade practice. The mill owners took advantage of this and fixed the prices at which sugar could be sold in the market. Simultaneously, they controlled the amount of sugar that was released from their mills to avoid an oversupply of the product. The syndicate worked and the mills made an enormous profit. The crisis for Gujarmal for that season was over.

By the time the next season of sugarcane crushing started, the sugar industry in India had matured and stabilized. The syndication of sugar had not gone down well with the common man and certainly not with the farmers. It was believed that it was only the mill owners who benefited from the policy of the government to control the import of sugar. To address the problems of the farmers, Sugarcane Development Cooperative Societies were formed across the sugarcane-growing areas. The farmers in a particular area were organized to be part of one cooperative society. The cooperative society could sell the sugarcane only to identified mills that fell in their area. The supply to the mills was regulated by the officers of the cooperative. The smart factory owners immediately realized the importance of these societies. They realized that instead of dealing with the farmers to buy their produce, the mill owners would have to deal with the cooperatives. To build a relationship with the cooperatives, the mill owners started paying a commission of 1 per cent to them. The cooperatives were happy with this arrangement and the money thus collected was used to repair and expand the road network in these areas. The farmers also benefited from being part of the cooperatives as they were assured of a fixed price for their produce.

In his area, Gujarmal took the lead in dealing with the cooperatives. He ensured that the road network to his mill from the nearby farms was improved. While he had the good of the farmers in mind, Gujarmal was also preparing for the township, which would have more mills soon. The work to build the township had been progressing. It had been built in a linear grid pattern, parallel to the railway line. The main road was the central grid line of the township. The residential units were all on one side of the main road and the factory was on the other side. The newer factories planned would also be across the road from the residential areas. Along with the residential units, Gujarmal had also planned a business area in the form of shops. The box-like shops were all lined along both sides of the main road.

In 1938, Gujarmal organized a water supply system—a network of pipes—for the residential complexes built for the workers of the mill. Medical facilities for the workers were expanded by employing more doctors. By now other smaller retail businesses were thriving in the township. There were over 5,000 workers employed in the mill and that meant a large number of residents in the township. These residents had requirements for daily needs and other products. Other shops selling products for the residents were allowed to be set up. By popular demand, the medical facilities, which were free for the workers and their families, were thrown open to outsiders as well. Gujarmal thus continued the philanthropic activities in his township as well.

As he saw the township growing in front of his eyes, Gujarmal could not help but feel a deep sense of satisfaction that the first steps towards the achievement of his dream had been taken by him. When he had left Patiala, he had wanted to leave behind the hedonistic lifestyle, the arbitrary rule based on the whims of one man and the arrogance of the ruler. However, he had spent his life in Patiala. Without him realizing it, he did carry some of the Patiala values with him to Begumabad. A sense of ownership over his township had already taken root within Gujarmal. He did look at all the workers and their families as 'his' people—much like the maharaja may have done with the people in his riyasat. Gujarmal also demanded unconditional loyalty from his workers—loyalty to him and loyalty to the work. Work had to come before family for everyone who worked for him. And Gujarmal ran his township and his work, even his family, with strict discipline.

Philanthropy had always been part of his character and now he institutionalized it. The factory, and every factory going forward, had to pay 10 per cent of their profits to the philanthropic trust. This 10 per cent was rooted in the concept of dasvandh—prevalent in the Sikh community. Dasvandh or dasaundh literally means a 'tenth part' and refers to the practice of donating 10 per cent of the harvest or profit towards the common resources of the community. This is also referred to as daan or charity. Gujarmal had been influenced by the practice of dasvandh and made it part of his current, and all future, businesses. The 10 per cent of the profits was ploughed back into building infrastructure and setting up services like dispensaries, schools, dharamshalas, temples, gardens—all for the good of the people.

The township, thus, was taking shape well. However, there was one problem that persisted. The sugar mill operated only during the sugarcane crushing season. Thus, the workers were not employed the full year round. Gujarmal knew that his dream of establishing an efficient industrial township would not take off with only one seasonal mill. To be a thriving industrial township, he needed more factories and mills. Hence, he started looking for the next business opportunity.

***

Gujarmal had been keen to set up a vanaspati manufacturing factory since 1929. He had tried to set it up in Patiala, but the administration had not given him permission. Again, in Calcutta his first thought had been to set up a vanaspati factory, but his mind changed after the government had increased the import duty on sugar. It was, therefore, natural that vanaspati manufacturing came up in his mind once again. It would be a product that could be manufactured all year round. And the time was also right to produce vanaspati.

M/s Lever Brothers (now Unilever) was the largest seller of vanaspati in India under the brand name Dalda. In those days, there was a Dutch company called Dada & Co. that imported the product from Holland. They had started importing in the early 1900s as they saw a growing market in India. Pure ghee was expensive, and people found it difficult to buy it for daily use. Vanaspati—hydrogenated fat—was made to look and feel like pure ghee. Lever Brothers sold the imported product and, to reflect their ownership, added the letter L to the name Dada—hence Dalda. In a bold marketing move, Lever advertised their product as Dalda—vanaspati ghee. The association of the product with ghee worked and it became a money-spinner for Lever Brothers. They had even set up a factory in Sewri, Bombay to manufacture Dalda in India.

Gujarmal decided to finally set up his vanaspati factory in Begumabad. He ordered the machines from Europe and, despite the raging world war, the machines were delivered on time. In June 1939, the factory of Modi Vanaspati Manufacturing Company was inaugurated. While Gujarmal was delighted at his new factory, he was not so happy at the birth of his third child in May 1939. The third child of Dayawati and Gujarmal was again a daughter, who was named Rajeshwari. Gujarmal, being the traditional and orthodox Hindu that he was, was keen to have a son to take his legacy forward. The inauguration of the new factory took his mind away from these domestic matters.

The vanaspati factory started producing and the product was sold across the country under the brand Kotogem. The product was accepted by the consumers, and the factory was running at full capacity. However, there were two large companies of Bombay that were not happy at Kotogem's and Gujarmal Modi's success.

The first company to feel threatened by Kotogem was Lever Brothers itself. Till Gujarmal started his national distribution of Kotogem, Dalda used to be the only vanaspati available nationally. Lever Brothers did not want their market share to go down due to a new competitor. They came to Gujarmal with a plan. Lever Brothers wanted Gujarmal to stop selling his vanaspati in the Indian market under the brand Kotogem. Instead, they wanted Gujarmal to become a supplier to their Sewri factory. The plan was that Lever Brothers would outsource the manufacturing of their Dalda product to Modi Vanaspati Manufacturing Company. Thus, the factory would continue to produce but sell only to Lever Brothers. 'We will make it worthwhile for you, Mr Modi,' said the senior officer of Lever Brothers. 'You will make far more money producing vanaspati for us than you will if you sell it yourself under your brand.'

Gujarmal looked at the officer and shook his head. 'Maybe you do not know but I am establishing an industrial township here. Products made here will be sold all over India under my brand. This is my dream and no amount of money will dazzle me enough to give up my dream,' explained Gujarmal.

The officers of Lever Brothers were surprised. They did not expect a native Indian to refuse what they believed was a very generous offer. Not used to being refused, they got angry. 'If you think that you can compete with us in the market, think again, Mr Modi,' raged the senior officer. 'We will wipe you off the market. You will be sorry that you refused our offer. Not only will you have to shut down your vanaspati factory, but you will be forced to sell your sugar mill as well.'

'Be that as it may,' replied Gujarmal calmly, 'God is with me and I know that he will not let me come to any harm. Do your best, sir.' He bid goodbye to the officers. He knew, however, that he would have to be ready for a fight in the market.

Lever Brothers initiated their action against Kotogem by starting a price war. They started selling Dalda to the distributors at a greatly discounted rate in the markets of Meerut, Ghaziabad, Hapur and other adjoining areas of Begumabad. Lever Brothers believed that Gujarmal would be unable to sell Kotogem in these markets. However, Gujarmal had been prepared for a price war since the visit of the Lever officers. He also knew that Lever Brothers sold ten times the quantity in these markets as compared to Kotogem. On the other hand, Kotogem sold lesser quantities compared to Dalda, and if Gujarmal dropped the prices, the loss would be much less. Thus, he calculated that the loss that Lever Brothers would incur due to the heavy discounting would be ten times the loss that Kotogem would incur. He readied himself and his people for a price war.

Gujarmal decided on a two-pronged strategy to take on Lever Brothers. One, he reduced the supply in the markets around Begumabad by 30 per cent and increased it in the other areas accordingly. Next, in the adjoining areas, where Dalda was sold at a discount, not only did he match the discount, he even gave a 5 per cent further discount if the distributors bought large quantities. His calculation was simple. If Lever Brothers matched the discount, their losses would go up even more. On the other hand, if Lever Brothers did not match Kotogem's price, Gujarmal's product would get sold out.

His plan was a success. Kotogem continued to sell in these markets. Lever Brothers, on the other hand, started incurring major losses due to their heavily discounted prices. In less than a year, Lever Brothers could not sustain the losses and went back to the normal pricing. Kotogem, too, stopped the discounting, which increased the margins, and the profit for Modi Vanaspati went up sharply.

While the matter of Lever Brothers was settled in the market, the other company took their matter to court. The Tatas had a brand of ghee with a name similar to Kotogem and they accused Gujarmal of copyright violation. Gujarmal explained to the Tatas that he had chosen the name Kotogem due to the fact that vanaspati used cotton seed oil as an ingredient. Hence, he played on the word 'cotton' and got his brand name. The Tatas were not convinced and threatened to take Gujarmal to court. Gujarmal was sure of his own case and told them to go ahead. The matter went to court and the lower courts in Bombay dismissed it. The Tatas persisted and took the matter to the Bombay High Court. The matter in this higher court also went in Gujarmal's favour.

Free from the worries of Lever Brothers and Tatas fighting him, Gujarmal concentrated on the vanaspati factory. Due to the world war, the import of hydrogenated oil had come down as the supply lines were affected. The demand was increasing, however, in the Indian market. Thus, the factory could not produce vanaspati fast enough to meet the demand of the market. Unlike the sugar mills, which had seen a couple of difficult years, the vanaspati factory started generating profits right from its first year.

***

The increasing wealth of the empire did not manifest itself in the lifestyle led by the Modi family. Gujarmal and Dayawati lived well but not ostentatiously. When people who did not know them met them, they realized that Gujarmal was not poor, but the extent of his wealth could not be ascertained by the clothes he wore or the food he ate. Sometimes it led to embarrassing situations. The wedding of a maternal second cousin was one such occasion.

The cousin was getting married to a girl from Calcutta. Even though the Modi family was a Marwari family, the Punjabi influence was strong among them as Gujarmal had grown up in Patiala. He dressed in long flowing kurtas, churidars and jootis—much like the gentry of Punjab. Their interactions with each other and with others were a bit rustic.

When the baraat reached Calcutta and the bride's father interacted with Gujarmal and his brothers, he was a little disturbed at what he saw. He took the Modi family to be a bunch of unsophisticated people. The bride's father extended the logic and believed that Gujarmal and his brothers were not well-off either. Since the Modi family was part of the baraat, the bride's family had no choice but to look after them and give them good hospitality, but their interactions made it clear that they thought that the Modis were below them in wealth and status.

Calcutta was a thriving city and under the British influence. People of Calcutta considered themselves cultured and sophisticated. The bride's Marwari family was rich too. They thought that the Modis were a bunch of poor village yokels. Gujarmal was quick to pick up on the signs but chose to keep quiet. He thought that there would be no interactions with the Calcutta family once the Modi family went back to Patiala and Begumabad; thus, he thought he could ignore the subtle putting down by the bride's family.

It was the morning of the day of departure of the baraat from Calcutta. One ceremony remained. This was the ceremony of the bride's father giving the bridegroom a final shagun—money or gift for the road. The bride's father gave the bridegroom ₹1 lakh as the shagun. As he handed over the thick wad of notes to the groom, the bride's father looked at Gujarmal slyly. 'See, I am giving one lakh rupees to your cousin,' he said, gesturing towards Gujarmal to come closer to see.

It was as if the bride's father was telling Gujarmal to come and have a look at what ₹1 lakh looked like. The implication could not be clearer. The bride's father believed that Gujarmal had not seen this amount of money before and was, therefore, inviting him to see it for himself.

Gujarmal calmly went towards the bride's father and his cousin. He nodded to the father and gestured to the bridegroom to hand over the money to him. As his cousin gave him the bundle of notes, Gujarmal did not even look at the money. Instead, he called out to one of his munims, who was part of the baraat.

'Here, take this,' Gujarmal instructed the munim. 'Do you see that dharamshala there?' he asked the munim, pointing to the far end of the road. A building housing a yatri dharamshala stood there. The munim nodded.

'Take this and give it to them and say we've sent it for them. We've come to Calcutta for an auspicious occasion. At such a time, we have to donate to the needy. Go and tell them that this is from the Modi family,' Gujarmal continued.

As the bride's father looked on with a stunned expression, Gujarmal beckoned another munim of his, who came scurrying fast. 'Munim, please ensure that my cousin gets two lakh rupees before he reaches home. One lakh that I sent to the dharamshala and one lakh from me as a shagun for him to start his new life,' Gujarmal instructed in a loud voice.

The bride's family could only look on without quite comprehending what had passed. The bride's father, though, understood the message clearly. The message was: 'Don't go by our outward appearances and don't treat us badly.'

The ₹2 lakh that were given to the cousin did not cause a dent in Gujarmal's wealth. The vanaspati factory was generating large profits.

The vanaspati factory also gave rise to Gujarmal's third factory. Oil sludge was one of the waste products of the vanaspati manufacturing process. This sludge was a raw material in the manufacturing of carbolic soap. Gujarmal set up his third factory, Modi Soap Works, in 1940 and started selling the washing clothes soap under the brand of Modi No. 1.

The year 1940 proved fortunate for Gujarmal as his first son was born in August. Dayawati and Gujarmal were ecstatic and believed that Bhagwan Krishna had blessed them as the son was born a day after the festival of Janmashtami. The newborn boy was named Krishna Kumar. The Modi family, finally, had an heir. Gujarmal, at the age of thirty-eight years, was finally able to shrug off the invisible burden he had been carrying on his shoulders for more than twenty years—that of not fathering a son.

***

Modi No. 1 soon became one of the largest-selling carbolic soaps for washing clothes. Gujarmal, now, wanted to set up a toilet soap factory. The only problem was that the process and ingredients used to manufacture toilet soap were different from that of the washing clothes soap. And Gujarmal did not have any knowledge of it. He had initially thought that he would ask one of the toilet soap manufacturers to give him the details. But Gujarmal's reputation as an astute and successful industrialist had started growing and no toilet soap manufacturer was willing to share the details. They were afraid of having Gujarmal as a competitor.

Gujarmal would not let these matters come in the way of his ambition. He had a friend in Banaras who manufactured toilet soap and Gujarmal went off to the river-city. His friend, too, found an excuse to keep Gujarmal away from the factory. Undeterred, Gujarmal went to Calcutta, where he thought that his friend Bajoria could help him gain access to a toilet soap factory. Bajoria tried but was unsuccessful. Gujarmal was at his wits' end. Unwilling to give up on his dream, he thought of using a different approach to get access to a toilet soap factory.

He took a car and started driving around the industrial area of Calcutta. It was summer and the temperatures were high. In 1940, there were no air-conditioned cars. Sweating profusely, Gujarmal stopped in front of a toilet soap factory, went in and asked for water. Luckily the owner, Sunder Lal, was in the factory and he welcomed Gujarmal and offered him a glass of water. Sitting in the owner's office, the two businessmen started talking. Gujarmal introduced himself as a resident of Begumabad, where he had sugar, vanaspati and carbolic soap factories.

'Oh, that's good to know. We manufacture soap here too, but we manufacture toilet soap,' said Sunder Lal.

'Toilet soap? Really?' said Gujarmal with an innocent expression. 'Do we make toilet soap in India? I thought that toilet soap was only imported.'

'No, no ... of course we manufacture toilet soap here. Come, I will show you,' said Sunder Lal proudly.

'That would be good. I did not know that making toilet soap was possible in India,' Gujarmal continued to pretend.

Sunder Lal summoned his chemist, Das Gupta, and asked him to give Gujarmal a tour of the toilet soap factory.

As Gujarmal and Das Gupta went around the factory, Gujarmal keenly watched the processes and asked many questions. The chemist thought that Gujarmal was his boss's good friend and gave him detailed answers. Gujarmal stopped at a place where the oil was being boiled in large vats. He saw some white substance being added to the boiling oil.

'What are you adding here?' asked Gujarmal.

'This is tallow. We are adding tallow to the soap mixture,' replied Das Gupta.

'What is tallow?' asked Gujarmal. He had some idea but wanted to validate it.

'It is a hard, fatty substance made from rendered animal fat,' replied Das Gupta.

'Are you the only ones who add tallow?' continued Gujarmal.

'No, every toilet soap factory does it,' replied Das Gupta.

Gujarmal was shell-shocked. 'B-b ... but ... but all advertisements for all toilet soaps say that they are without any animal fat. And isn't tallow beef fat? How can you put beef fat into soaps that are used by Hindus? Even I use soaps. I will have to stop using them,' Gujarmal went on in a rush. He asked Das Gupta if soap could be made without any tallow.

'Technically, soap can be made but without any tallow, or any fatty substance, the soap will stay soft and it will not be possible for us to shape it. We know that we don't tell anyone that we are adding beef tallow. That is why we don't let anyone enter our factories. You are a friend of our owner. Therefore, I am telling you this,' explained Das Gupta. 'So, no, you can't make toilet soap without any tallow.'

'I will do it,' asserted Gujarmal.

Das Gupta knew that Gujarmal had a vanaspati factory. 'So, if you will not add tallow, will you add vanaspati?' he laughed and asked Gujarmal.

'Yes, I will,' replied Gujarmal with confidence.

'But the soap will be so expensive!' exclaimed Das Gupta.

'Yes, it will be expensive, no doubt,' replied Gujarmal. 'But our sentiments are worth more than money. How can I cheat all the Hindus and give them a product that is non-vegetarian?'

Das Gupta was swept away by Gujarmal's passion. When Gujarmal asked him if he would consider leaving his present job to come and help him set up a toilet soap factory, Das Gupta readily agreed. With Das Gupta as the main chemist, Gujarmal added an extension to the existing carbolic soap factory and started producing a toilet soap called Prefect.

Another product meant another factory, which further meant more workers and their families came to reside in Begumabad. The township was growing each year. More workers meant more houses needed to be built. Gujarmal wanted all his workers to live a life of dignity. Living in a pucca house with the basic amenities was part of this life with dignity. He felt a sense of ownership for all who came to work in his factories. He had established a school and hospital in the township and had created a few parks for recreation. A large temple had also been built. The workers and their families reciprocated this love and affection, and looked upon Dayawati and Gujarmal as the first couple of their township.

Gujarmal had four factories now. The revenues and profits had grown. His lifestyle, however, did not change. The words of his mother kept coming back to him. 'Son, remember that you are a mere custodian of the wealth earned. You are a trustee. Do not get attached to the wealth,' Rukmini Devi's voice echoed in his mind. He, too, believed in the concept of trusteeship. Thus, even though the wealth of the business increased, his personal wealth did not. All the shares of the businesses were held in a trust. All assets of the business—the land, factories, other buildings—were owned by the trust. Even the house Gujarmal and Dayawati lived in did not belong to them—it belonged to the company. Further, Gujarmal set up many philanthropic trusts which focused on a variety of charitable activities.

Business opportunities kept knocking on Gujarmal's door and he answered each one of them. In 1941, a tin factory was set up to provide tin containers for Kotogem. Soon thereafter, he set up an oil mill to provide the raw material for his soap factories. While he was happy in Begumabad, he worried about the business in Patiala, which was not doing well in his absence. Even though he wanted to, he could not find time to leave Begumabad and go to Patiala. He requested his younger half-brother, Harmukhrai Modi, to help him manage the Patiala business.

***

By now the Second World War was raging and threatening to engulf the world. Europe and England were already severely affected by Hitler's army. The British Army needed arms and armaments, which was being handled by their government. But an army cannot march on empty stomachs, and carrying food items was not an easy task. Meanwhile the British government had heard that the Germans had perfected the art of carrying dehydrated food. The soldiers had packs of dehydrated vegetables which did not weigh much. When the soldiers wanted to eat, all they had to do was add hot water to the dehydrated food. Voila. They had hot food.

The government in India wanted to explore possibilities of manufacturing dehydrated food in India. The senior general of the British Army in India called for a meeting of major industrialists. At the meeting he explained the concept of the German dehydrated vegetables and asked if any of the industrialists present could take on the challenge to start producing them in India. All the people present there looked at each other and shook their heads. No one had heard of the technique and no one believed that he could take on the responsibility. The general was visibly upset and merely said, 'I am greatly disappointed. I had thought that you all had great initiative. But I was wrong.'

Gujarmal, who was also present in the meeting, did not like the general's words. He stood up and said, 'General, I will take on the responsibility of making dehydrated food.'

Surprised, the general looked up at Gujarmal and asked, 'Are you sure you will be able to do it?'

'I am sure that I will do it,' replied Gujarmal with conviction.

'How? None of your friends seem to be able to,' asked the general.

'I don't know how I will do it yet,' replied Gujarmal candidly. 'But one thing I know for sure is that there is no task that cannot be completed—all you have to do is try and work hard. I will do both.' The general was delighted and gave Gujarmal one month to get back to him.

Gujarmal hadn't the foggiest idea about how to go about setting up a manufacturing process for dehydrated food. But he did not stress over it. Whenever he was faced with a problem that he could not solve, he would sleep over it. So it was with this problem. Gujarmal meditated about the problem each day before sleeping. He had started keeping sheets of paper and a pencil near his bedside. This was to enable him to pen down his thoughts and ideas from his dreams.

He meditated about the problem each night and then one night he found the solution in his dreams. In his dream it was as if he were being taken on a tour of a factory in Germany. A voice in his dream kept telling him to see the machinery and the plant layout of the factory carefully. The dream was crystal clear. He woke up and immediately wrote down what he had seen and even drew rough sketches of the machinery he had seen.

The next day he asked the carpenters to make wooden models based on the sketches. Gujarmal tested the models, made corrections where he found necessary and then got them made in iron. He began experimenting using the iron models. Several tonnes of potatoes were ordered, peeled, cut and then boiled. After that they were dehydrated. Gujarmal found that 100 mann of potatoes when dehydrated weighed only 10 mann. He was able to bring down the weight by over 90 per cent. He knew that he could deliver the promise made to the general.

In May 1941, Modi Food Products was launched. Dehydrated vegetables were produced and packed for the British Army. The general was delighted and brought a delegation of high-ranking army officials to visit the factory. Modi Food Products worked at full capacity as the demand from the army kept increasing. This successful company was separated from the parent company of Modi Sugar Mills and was taken public in December 1941. At the same time, Gujarmal set up another factory called Modi Supplies Corporation Limited to supply dry fruit to the British Army. Supplying rations and other consumables to the British Army was not new to Gujarmal. After all, his family had made its money from supplying to the British Army. He tapped into that expertise and grew the business manifold in no time. A factory to make masalas was also set up soon after.

Gujarmal realized that he could not handle the expanding business by himself. He was nearly forty years old and his son was still a toddler. Gujarmal, therefore, asked his half-brother Kedarnath Modi to help him. Kedarnath relocated to Begumabad and started working alongside his elder brother. Gujarmal told Kedarnath very proudly that the vegetable dehydration plant was the first of its kind in India. The process was yet unpatented in the country. Gujarmal applied for a patent for the process and, once he received it, presented it to the government so that they could use it for the greater good. Everyone, including the government officials, was surprised that the patent was being given without any charge. Gujarmal told them that he looked at it as part of his philanthropic activities as the patent would be used to produce food items for the army.

Gujarmal, by 1942, had established schools for the children of the workers, many canteens for wholesome vegetarian food for the workers and their families, charitable hospitals and temples. He had also established a school for girls, Modi Putri Pathshaala, in early 1942. All this work was not going unnoticed by the government. Delhi had been surprised and happy at

Gujarmal's gesture of donating the patent. The government had also heard about the expanding businesses of Gujarmal. It was decided in Delhi to honour Gujarmal with the title of Rai Bahadur.

The title of Rai Bahadur was a coveted and prestigious one. It was awarded by the British government to Indians to recognize the work done by them. Not only was it a great honour for the individual but it was considered a great recognition for the family, district and state to which the individual belonged. The title of Rai Bahadur was accompanied by a medal featuring a loop for the ribbon, a British Crown with a laurel wreath below it, two circles with a side portrait of George V within the inner circle and the title itself engraved within the two circles. All this was surmounted by a five-pointed star.

It was a matter of great celebration, therefore, in the Modi household as the news of Gujarmal being awarded the title of Rai Bahadur spread. The honour was even more significant as Gujarmal was only forty years old. The joy was doubled as Multanimal, too, had been awarded the same title a few years ago. Two members of the same family being awarded the Rai Bahadur honour was not common. The entire township in Begumabad erupted with joy. The workers felt that each one of them had received the honour. Houses were lit up in the evening with lamps and people mingled with each other in the streets, distributing sweets. The township was also celebrating the birth of the fourth child of Dayawati and Gujarmal—a girl. The daughter was named Urmila Devi.

Gujarmal and Dayawati were firmly established in Begumabad by now. The visits to Patiala had become infrequent. Gujarmal had a routine of sorts by now. He would get up early and go for an hour-long walk in Begumabad. A couple of clerks, each carrying a notebook and pencil, would walk behind Gujarmal as he took his customary long strides. The residents of Begumabad soon realized that if they wanted to speak with Gujarmal, they could do so during that morning walk. But they also learnt that while Gujarmal was happy to talk to them, they had to follow the strict protocol. Gujarmal was not part of any royal family but people in Begumabad treated him like a king and he had come to accept it as normal. Thus people desirous of speaking with Gujarmal needed to approach the clerks walking behind him, who in turn would whisper to their boss.

On his part, Gujarmal listened to all those who wanted to speak with him and gave instructions to one of the clerks, who wrote it down in his notebook. After the walk, Gujarmal would do body-building exercises. He was also a good wrestler and did not shy away from challenging anyone to meet him in the akhara. Few people, however, took up the challenge. After the exercises, Gujarmal would get himself massaged liberally with oil. After his bath he would pray and then go to the office. But no matter how much work he had, Gujarmal would not sacrifice his daily game of bridge. He was passionate about the card game, as was Dayawati. At night after dinner there would be an hour-long puja in the Modi home. Everyone at home, including the children, was expected to be part of the puja.

News about the philanthropic work being done in Begumabad had spread to other parts of the country. People in Mahendragarh, erstwhile Kanoud, wrote to Gujarmal to keep them in his mind as well. They reminded him that his great-grandfather had started his business journey from Kanoud. Gujarmal readily agreed and asked them what was needed. The answer was not slow in coming. They wanted a high school in their district. There was only one middle school catering to the many villages in Mahendragarh. The villagers wanted their children to study at least till high school. In 1943, Gujarmal set up a large school in Mahendragarh and named it Yadavendra Multanimal Higher Secondary School.

# 9

# *From Begumabad to Modinagar*

THE years after 1942 saw Gujarmal setting up one factory after another and growing the township to a larger size. It had only been nine years since he set up his first factory. He may have been in his early forties but he went about his work with the energy of a younger man. Each factory that he built was large, spacious and with proper light and ventilation so that the workers could work properly. While there were no licences and other controls, transportation and communication were the main constraints faced by Gujarmal and other industrialists of that era. Hauling and bringing construction material remained a challenge due to the inadequate road network. As Begumabad was near a railway line, Gujarmal was able to manage the logistics better than some others who were setting up factories in remote areas. Communication with the suppliers and vendors, too, was not simple. Telephone—only landlines at that time—was a rarity. Letters and telegrams were the most common method of communicating with people. Gujarmal took all this in his stride and focused on building more factories. He had taken the words of his mother very seriously and was focused on being a karma yogi.

Among all the flurry of activities, Gujarmal remained true to the commitment of helping others. The trusts and charities were the main vehicles of the philanthropic activities. However, they were no substitutes for the personal philanthropic actions carried out by both Gujarmal and Dayawati.

One morning on his routine walk, in the summer of 1943, Gujarmal noticed a callow young man hovering around, as if gathering courage to come up to the industrialist.

'Who is this fellow and why is he hanging around here?' Gujarmal turned to the clerk and asked.

The clerk told his boss that the young man, named Kishore, belonged to a village in the neighbourhood. 'Sir, this boy Kishore is educated but has been unable to find a job. He tried but has been unsuccessful at finding any kind of job,' replied the clerk. Kishore had become despondent and had lost the will to live. He wanted to commit suicide but a friend talked him out of it. The same friend told Kishore about Gujarmal. 'I am sure that if you are able to meet Rai Bahadur, he will give you a job,' the friend had said.

Kishore had made his way to Begumabad and was hovering around Gujarmal in the hope of being able to talk to him. He could not, however, gather up his courage to actually speak up. Kishore, therefore, started following Gujarmal as he walked, hoping that he would catch his eye.

As the clerk finished telling Gujarmal about the young boy, Gujarmal stopped and gestured for Kishore to come forward.

As the boy came forward hesitatingly, Gujarmal realized that Kishore was close to his breaking point. 'What is the matter, son?' asked Gujarmal in his booming voice. Kishore told his story and even confessed that he had lost his will to live. As he heard this, Gujarmal got agitated. 'What is this nonsense about taking your own life? Don't you know that it is a sin? Promise me that you will never, ever talk like this,' said Gujarmal. Kishore made the promise. 'Good. Come to my office in the afternoon. We will figure something out for you,' promised Gujarmal in return. Kishore was given a job in the sugar mill and he went on to establish a household and a family in Begumabad.

Meanwhile, Gujarmal was on an expanding spree. In 1943, he established a biscuit factory which was soon followed by Modi Confectionary Works, which produced candies for children. By now Gujarmal had nine separate businesses, each of which was doing well. The year 1943 was good for Gujarmal for one more reason. On 31 May 1943, Dayawati and Gujarmal were blessed with their second son. This boy was named Vinay Kumar. The same year, almost as if to celebrate the second son, Gujarmal set up a charitable trust and named it after his father. Rai Bahadur Multanimal Modi Charitable Trust was set up with a sum of ₹10 lakh. The Modi mansion in Haridwar was also gifted to the trust.

Gujarmal had established an oil mill in 1941 to cater to the needs of his soap factory. Now he needed another one to supply to his vanaspati factory. Thus, in 1944, Gujarmal set up Modi Oil Mills and this produced mustard and peanut oil. This oil mill became the tenth business for Gujarmal. He realized that he needed additional hands. He had already brought Kedarnath, his oldest half-brother, into the business. Now he requested Kedarnath's younger brother, Madanlal Modi, to come in and manage the new oil mill.

Gujarmal, like most industrialists of his time, set up his factories in an opportunistic manner rather than in a strategic manner. India was a poor country and manufacturing was not well developed. Further, the consumer market was not well developed; most of the products were sold like commodities. Thus, in a way it was easy to set up a factory because the industrialist knew that the product he manufactured would sell. Thus, Gujarmal set up factories from sugar to vanaspati to soap to oil to biscuits to tin—a diverse set seemingly unconnected without any strategy.

The strategy, however, was clear and long term. Instead of focusing on the specific products, the industrialists in general, and Gujarmal in particular, had a strategy for establishing a business for the long term. Gujarmal wanted to create a legacy for the future generations. India was not an independent nation yet and therefore nation-building was not high among the objectives. Once India did become free of British rule, nation-building jumped right to the top three reasons for Gujarmal.

***

Begumabad had ten thriving factories by now. The township was slowly growing to be a small town. Gujarmal was falling short of land to build new housing complexes. As the number of workers coming into Begumabad to work in the existing and new factories was increasing, the town was running out of residential quarters for them. It was at this time that Gujarmal's foresight came in handy. In 1943, Gujarmal had spent ₹25,000 to build a sainik bhawan (house for soldiers) for the army men in

Meerut. The local commander had publicly thanked Gujarmal. Since then, the relationship between them had developed further. Thus, when Gujarmal wanted some land for building residential quarters, he thought of the tract of land just across the road from his sugar mill. The tract of land belonged to the army and was a designated military camp area. Gujarmal went to the commander and expressed his desire to buy the military camp area from the army.

'But you already own all of Begumabad and then some more,' said the commander and laughed.

Gujarmal replied seriously, 'Sir, it is indeed true that I own a large part of the land here but it is not land in my name. It belongs to the company. And the land is used to build structures for the benefit of the workers.' He went on to explain that he wanted his workers to live with dignity in proper houses. Thus, he had built these large housing complexes. 'But now I have so many businesses and factories and more workers come in every day. And I need to build more housing quarters to accommodate them.'

'You are a good man, Gujarmal,' replied the commander. 'I know that you will use the land for the benefit of the workers. I will recommend that the army sells the land to you.' Gujarmal was delighted and started work on yet another housing complex for his workers. Along with a housing complex, he also started work on another dispensary for the town. The Modi High School had teachers who were committed and professional. One of the reasons for this was the fact that Gujarmal had created an exclusive residential complex for the teachers. Good teachers attracted better students, from Begumabad and adjacent areas. To enable more outstation students to benefit from the education being provided, Gujarmal started work on a new students' hostel, which was completed in 1945.

In 1945, Dayawati and Gujarmal were blessed with another daughter. They named her Pramila. The year 1945 also saw the end of the Second World War. While it brought peace to the world and the soldiers returned to their respective homes, Gujarmal had to shut down two of his factories. Modi Food Products providing dehydrated food items to the army and Modi Supplies Corporation which supplied dry fruit to the army had to be shut down as the orders from the army stopped. No longer did the army need their soldiers to eat dehydrated food. However, the government recognized the contribution of Gujarmal in the war through these two factories and wanted to felicitate him. The government organized a procession in Meerut which was a major army cantonment. Gujarmal was made to sit atop a decorated elephant. While he was given the pride of place by being seated alone on the elephant, the additional district magistrate and the tehsildar (a senior officer in the government) sat together on another elephant. Behind these two elephants was a procession. The procession was led by the army band, marching smartly through the city. The residents came out of their houses and some went on the terraces to watch. They threw flowers on to the parade. It was a great honour for Gujarmal and the Modi family.

Not satisfied with felicitating Gujarmal publicly, the government wanted to bestow knighthood on him. They wanted his title to change from Rai Bahadur to Sir. As the talk of the impending knighthood reached Multanimal, he cautioned his son against it. 'These Britishers will go sooner or later. It will be better if you ask them for an Indian title,' advised

Multanimal. Gujarmal understood the nuances and requested the governor accordingly. The governor was sympathetic and promised that he would speak to the Viceroy about it.

Gujarmal was already a Rai Bahadur. A higher Indian title that could be given to him was Raja Bahadur. The Viceroy agreed in principle but highlighted a technical problem. The title of Raja Bahadur was given to Indians who were big zamindars. The zamindars, typically, owned many villages in an area. Gujarmal, though a big industrialist, did not own land nor any village personally. All the land belonged to the companies and trusts. Gujarmal did not even own the house he lived in. Thus, under the guidelines laid down, the Viceroy was finding it difficult to bestow the title of Raja Bahadur on Gujarmal, even though the governor and the Viceroy did sincerely want to felicitate Gujarmal. An innovative idea took shape in the governor's mind. He proposed that the township set up by Gujarmal be named Modinagar (Town of Modi). This way Gujarmal, as the founder of Modinagar, could qualify for the title of Raja Bahadur.

Thus in 1945, Modinagar was born. The post office, the railway station, the bus station and the police station all changed their addresses as well. They were all now in Modinagar. It was a huge moment in the life of the entire Modi family. The residents of Begumabad, now Modinagar, were also delighted. The day the change of name was announced, it was as if Diwali had come to the town early. All houses were lit up with earthen diyas. People wore their best clothes and went to each other's houses to wish each other. Gujarmal and Dayawati, too, came out and thanked the residents who had gathered in front of their house. The celebrations continued all through the night in Modinagar.

There were not many examples of industrialists having a town named after them. Jamshedpur and Walchandnagar were the two other cities that were named after their founders. Gujarmal joined an elite and exclusive list of industrialists and his reputation spread wider.

Once Begumabad became Modinagar officially, the governor proposed once again to the Viceroy that Gujarmal be bestowed with the Raja Bahadur title. The technical difficulty had been taken care of. As the process for approval started, there was another development in the Indian political world.

After the success of the Quit India Movement in 1942, the British government had realized that they needed to give more autonomy to the Indian government. In fact, Indians had agreed to support the British Army in the Second World War only because of the promise of more autonomy made to them. Thus, after the end of the war, elections to the provincial legislature were held followed by elections to the constituent assembly. An interim Indian government was formed in 1946. One of the decisions made by this government was to stop the practice of bestowing titles on to Indians. The interim government saw this practice as one that exemplified the master–servant relationship between the British and the Indians.

Caught in this development, which was completely out of the Viceroy's control, Gujarmal could not be conferred a higher title. The titles already bestowed, however, were allowed to stay. Rai Bahadur Gujarmal Modi could not get the title of Raja Bahadur. But he did have an entire city named after him.

Gujarmal was not unhappy at this development. When some of the senior members of the factory came to convey their disappointment at Gujarmal not getting the Raja Bahadur title, Gujarmal waved away their concerns. 'It is actually very fortunate,' he told the visitors. 'Raja Bahadur Gujarmal Modi may be forgotten a hundred years from now. But Modinagar is on the map and will always remain so. My name will be remembered for as long as Modinagar is in existence.'

The development in Modinagar took on a new pace as the residents were energized by the new name of their town. The government constituted a town area committee to look after public health, sanitation, lighting and other civic matters. As the founder of the town, Gujarmal was nominated to head the committee. He was later elected as the first chairman of the town area committee of Modinagar.

Multanimal was overjoyed, as was the entire Modi family. Having a town named after their family name was a great honour. To celebrate the honour, Gujarmal asked the Modi Charitable Trust to develop a large garden in Patiala along with a guest house for sadhus. He also asked the trust to establish a Sanskrit school in which students would be provided free clothes and food.

Refusing a glass of wine in 1932 had set off a chain of events for Gujarmal. Banished from the riyasat of Patiala, Gujarmal had decided to set up his own township. He had achieved it in merely thirteen years. Not only had he set up a township, it was now even named after him.

# 10

## *A Textile Mill Causes Problems*

IN 1946, Gujarmal wanted to expand his business by starting a textile mill. It was to be a large mill and would cost over ₹1 crore, which was an exceptional amount of money in 1946. However, as all businesses promoted by Gujarmal were doing well and earning good returns for the investors, he had no problem in securing funding for the cloth mill. With the money in the bank, the next item on the agenda was the acquisition of land for the mill. Gujarmal had his eye on a large piece of land owned by Gujjars in the neighbouring village of Sikri. He applied for permission to purchase the land and received the necessary approvals. He took possession of the land in June 1946.

The Gujjar landowners were not happy with the permission given by the British government to Gujarmal. They already had a history of confrontation with Gujarmal when, in 1933, they had tried to stop Modi Sugar Mill from being built by erecting a mud dam to prevent the drainage of rainwater from the mill area. Gujarmal's tact had saved the day, but the misgivings had continued to simmer. The rich landowners of Sikri village were also unhappy about losing their workforce to the mills of Modinagar.

Thirteen years later, when Gujarmal bought the land in Sikri for establishing a cloth mill, the villagers saw red. They saw it as a defeat in their battle with Gujarmal. True, they had received good money for their land but they had not wanted Gujarmal to buy it in the first place. They would have been happy to sell it to anyone else except Gujarmal. But the permission had been given and the deal was done. Some villagers looked around to seek support in their attempt to stop Gujarmal from establishing a factory on Sikri land.

Fortunately for them, they were able to get the support of some communist leaders who had gathered in Delhi around the same time. Leaders and workers of the communist party had convened in Delhi to take part in the railwaymen strike, which was launched as a protest against the government. Due to deft handling by the British government, the strike fizzled out. But it left the large number of workers and leaders, in Delhi for a confrontation, feeling a bit cheated. They had been primed by the leaders and their emotions were running high.

With the strike called off, a large group of protestors left Delhi and started on the highway that went through Modinagar, Meerut and onwards. Modinagar is almost halfway between the two cities and the group halted there.

It was a ragtag band of people who had been promised a good confrontation and, having been denied it in Delhi, were looking for it anywhere they could. In Modinagar, they saw a prosperous town with many factories and mills. The leaders of the group made enquiries and found out that the owner of the entire town and the businesses within was the Modi family. As communists, the group was opposed to capitalism. They wanted to make the capitalist Gujarmal pay. Some of the leaders went to Gujarmal and alleged that he was exploiting the workers in his factories. They then demanded ₹5,000 and when Gujarmal, not succumbing to blackmail, refused, the communist leaders threatened to incite the Modi workers against the Modi brothers. Gujarmal told them to go ahead.

The group had got their confrontation and were energized into action. They organized loudspeakers and put them up outside the factories. They then started propaganda against Gujarmal and his factories. The loudspeakers proclaimed loudly that Gujarmal was a capitalist and that he was exploiting his workers. The loudspeakers further egged the workers to organize themselves and strike back at the factory owners. The Modinagar workers, who were by and large happy working for the Modi family, tried to overlook the propaganda and ignored the protestors. The communists felt frustrated at the lack of interest from the workers. 'We are fighting for your rights. Why will you not join us?' exasperated, they asked the workers. The workers went to Gujarmal, who asked them to continue their work in the usual manner. He also advised them to ignore the blaring loudspeakers.

Gujarmal lodged a complaint against the agitating crowd in the office of the district magistrate. As was the procedure, the complaint was forwarded to the new interim Indian government in Lucknow. The parliamentary secretary in the Ministry of Home Affairs was reported to have told the district magistrate that the new government was not in the business of appeasing and patronizing capitalists. The district magistrate was advised to ignore the matter and not be seen taking the side of the industrialist. When Gujarmal was told of the decision, he realized that he could not fight the government as well as the agitating communists together. He decided to wait and watch before precipitating any further action.

As he waited, the agitators gained strength. By now the farmers of the adjoining area who did not want their land to be used for a factory also joined them. The group started virulent propaganda against Gujarmal. One part of the group started a rumour that the new government had issued an order which entitled every farmer selling his sugarcane to the mills to free sugar. This free sugar was to be a tenth of the sugar produced by the mill from the sugarcane supplied by each farmer. The farmers decided to march to the sugar mill to claim their share of free sugar. The communists promised to help them.

On 26 June, a large group of farmers and communist agitators started marching towards Modi Sugar Mills. They had brought some students from Meerut College and made them join the march. They also got some children to intermingle in the crowd of marchers. As the crowd neared the mill, the agitators put the female students and the smaller children in the front. The crowd behind them consisted of the agitators and farmers armed with sticks.

Gujarmal had been seeing the build-up of the protestors. He had realized that the agitators wanted a physical altercation and violence. He sent a message to the mill officers to disarm the factory guards and wardens of the sugar mill. Gujarmal did not want any of his employees to start any altercation. The message that went from Gujarmal to all his workers, wardens and guards was to stay calm and not use physical violence of any kind, no matter what the provocation.

This foresight of Gujarmal proved useful. As he had feared, when the protestors reached the mill, the girls provoked the guards and wardens by slapping them and even threw their turbans on the ground. However, the guards and wardens stood firm and did not retaliate as they were under orders from Gujarmal. Frustrated, the protesters forced their way into the mill and vandalized the machinery and hit the workers. After that, the protestors went to the biscuit factory. Not only did they eat the biscuits, they threw the half-eaten biscuits on the ground and stamped on them. The sugar godown was looted and the protestors carried bags of sugar from there. However, in spite of intense provocation, the protestors could not incite violence from the workers nor from the factory guards.

Gujarmal feared the safety of his workers more than he feared the protestors. He ordered all mills and factories to be shut down and locked. The district magistrate could no longer ignore the violence and acts of agitation in areas under his watch.

The day after the protestors had entered the mills, the district magistrate came to Modinagar with a senior police officer and a small posse of armed policemen. The officers wanted to inspect the damage in the factories and take stock of the situation. The protestors heard about the inspection team and, emboldened by the previous day's events, reached the site again. Unmindful of the senior officer, the protestors gheraoed the government team. Some students manhandled the police officer, who was a Britisher. They snatched his cap and threw it on the ground before stamping on it. Another protestor snatched the baton of the British officer. Again, even in light of this intense provocation, the police officer refrained from giving the order to fire. With a new interim Indian government in place, he did not want to take any action that would not be liked by the new government. He did, however, round up the rowdy protestors and got them taken to the local police station, where they were placed in a lock-up.

The remaining protestors now moved en masse to the police station and demanded the release of their fellow agitators. When the police officer refused, the mob threatened to burn down the police station. The threat worked and the rowdy elements were released. The district magistrate and the police officer realized that the matter was getting out of hand and rushed back to Meerut. Though they had promised Gujarmal that they would return, they never did.

Meanwhile the protestors continued their acts of disruption. Even though all mills were shut down, the protestors put their own locks on all doors and gates of the mills. Roads were blocked so that students could not go to their classes. The agitators shut down the water supply of the town. The residents were all trapped inside their homes as no one wanted to take a chance and go outside to get caught in the protests.

When he saw that the district magistrate and the police officer had fled back to Meerut and not returned, Gujarmal realized that he could not depend on the local officials. He decided the time for wait-and-watch was over. He decided to take the matter into his own hands. He went to Lucknow to meet senior political leaders of the government.

Gujarmal had spent the last thirteen years focused on his businesses and factories. He was aware of the changing political environment and had started contributing financially to the Congress party, which was at the forefront of the Independence movement. His dealings with the government, till now, had led him to believe that the political leaders considered entrepreneurs vital to the growth of the country. True, India was not a free country but the 'masters' had let the spirit of capitalism flow. Gujarmal had missed reading the signs of the new interim government. He had missed understanding the socialistic mood of the new leaders fighting for independence. His visit to Lucknow was a wake-up call for him.

Modinagar was part of the United Provinces (later called Uttar Pradesh). After the British government had ordered new elections to the provincial legislatures in 1945, Congress had won a majority and Govind Ballabh Pant was the chief minister.

Once in Lucknow, Gujarmal met with the chief minister, the home minister—Rafi Ahmad Kidwai—and the industries minister—Kailashnath Katju. Gujarmal apprised them of the situation in Modinagar. He told them of the lackadaisical attitude of the local officers and of his frustration at the inaction.

'I can't understand why you are treating the protestors who have disrupted my entire town with kid gloves,' Gujarmal said, spreading his arms in frustration. 'Do you realize that the factories have not been able to function for days now?'

'But Gujarmal ji, we have to be careful about how we treat people,' said one officer of the ministry. 'We can't be seen siding with you. After all, you are a rich man, no?' He looked at Gujarmal with raised eyebrows.

'I am a rich man because I work hard and set up factories. If you want factories to shut down, it is better you tell me straight,' he said brusquely. 'I will shut them down immediately. This violence is not benefiting anyone.' He shifted agitatedly in his chair.

Though the thinking of the government was socialistic, it certainly did not want factories to be shut down. The state home minister, Rafi Ahmad Kidwai, summoned the police officer from Meerut and heard from him, first-hand, the entire matter. He was upset at the chaos created by the communist leaders and instructed the police officer to take the necessary action to get the situation under control. He then assured Gujarmal that the government did not want to shut down factories nor did they want to overrule all actions of the British government. Kidwai also told Gujarmal that the Congress knew that Gujarmal had donated generously to their party and that they would keep that in mind as well.

Armed with the assurances, Gujarmal returned to Modinagar. Law and order was restored and the protestors were driven out of town. The entire town and its residents heaved a sigh of relief as the factories reopened after ten days of shutdown.

***

Gujarmal returned from Lucknow a changed man. Literally. Gujarmal's normal attire used to be the traditional churidar pyjama, silk achkan with golden buttons and Jodhpuri safa. He had gone to Lucknow dressed in this manner. To him, this was nothing out of the ordinary. However, when he went to meet the leaders in the government offices, he found everyone there staring at him as if he were an animal out of a zoo. He could not understand the reason for this. It was only when he met Govind Ballabh Pant that he understood the reason. Pant told Gujarmal that the days of the zamindars and royals were over. The new India looked at them suspiciously. Pant further went on to say that while he knew that Gujarmal was a self-made man and did not belong to a royal family, his attire sent out a different message.

Gujarmal was an astute businessman. He realized that going forward he would have to deal with Indian politicians instead of the British ones. He, therefore, took Pant's advice seriously and decided to undergo a sartorial transformation. He decided to do away with the silk achkan and instead started wearing cotton kurtas and bandis (half-jackets). Instead of the safa, he started wearing a white Gandhi cap.

Gujarmal carried back another message from Lucknow. He now realized that the days of capitalism under the British government were soon going to be over. The interim government, both at the centre and in the provinces, had started a socialistic approach to business and businessmen. His conversation with Katju left a deep impression on Gujarmal. Katju reportedly told Gujarmal that the common man in India was developing a mistrust of the rich industrialists. Common Indians lived in poor conditions. When they saw the rich and ostentatious lifestyle of the industrialists and businessmen, the common man felt enraged. It was believed that the rich were exploiting the poor. Gujarmal was also told that once India was independent, it would be the government's endeavour to create some kind of equality by making the rich pay.

Gujarmal heard Katju and was quietly horrified at the thinking of the people in power. He had been a businessman all his life and firmly believed that the only way to pull people out of poverty was to give them good jobs so that they could earn enough money. But he was astute enough not to voice his opinion just then as he needed the fracas in Modinagar to be sorted out. But he did tell Katju how he had set up Modinagar and how the workers were looked after by the company. 'If you visit Modinagar, Katju Sahib, you will see that not all rich businessmen are the same,' said Gujarmal. He told Katju that he and his family lived in the same area as the workers. There was open interaction between the Modi family and the families of the workers. Gujarmal also gave details of the welfare work carried out by the Modi family for the residents of Modinagar. 'You should not believe what other people say, Katju Sahib. You should come and visit us yourself to see with your own eyes that I am telling the truth,' Gujarmal told Katju. Gujarmal returned to Modinagar with a promise made by Katju that he would soon visit Modinagar.

Back in Modinagar, with the matter with the communist protestors settled, Gujarmal had to look for a new piece of land for his textile mill. The distrust between the Gujjar community and the senior people of the Modi group had grown, and Gujarmal did not want to risk another blowout of any kind. Emotions were running high anyway due to the impending independence from the British. Gujarmal thought it was prudent to relocate the mill to another place where he would not face hostility from the locals. There was a barren piece of land near a village called Bisokhar. In fact, it was a much larger piece of land than the one in Sikri village. Since the land was barren and nothing was growing on it, the approvals came fast and there was no protest by the villagers. He already had the funding as his shares for this mill had been sold out within three days of a public offer. He had collected ₹1 crore for this mill.

By the time the work on the textile mill started, Gujarmal and Dayawati were blessed with another son. This son, born in October 1946, was named Satish Kumar.

The next year, 1947, was a momentous one for India. India became independent in August 1947 and over 200 years of the British Raj came to an end.

# 11

# *Learning to Do Business in Independent India*

INDEPENDENT India brought new hopes and joys for Indians. It also, however, brought pain and suffering to millions as Partition took place. Millions of Indians were uprooted and had to move across the border—Muslims from India moved to Pakistan and Hindus from across the new border moved to independent India. Undivided India had been a single, unified economic unit whose economy was based on inter-regional specialization and dependence. With a single stroke of the pen, this economic unit was divided into two unequal parts. The largest impact was felt in agriculture.

As a result of Partition, more than 80 per cent of the net sown area remained in India and the balance went to Pakistan. Though Pakistan received less agricultural land, the irrigation facilities in the new country were much better. Thus, a larger part of agricultural land in Pakistan (45 per cent) was served by irrigation works, and only a small part of agricultural land in India (18 per cent) was irrigated. Further, the irrigation works in India were largely 'defensive' or 'protective' in character—they were focused on warding off possible famines and not on increasing yield per acre. Partition, therefore, made the Indian farmer more dependent on the vagaries of rainfall and the monsoon. India had been deficient in foodgrains even before Partition. After Partition, however, this deficiency was aggravated. Taking away the amount of grain produced in the new country, Pakistan, there was a net loss of between 7–8 lakh tonnes of foodgrains annually for India. This foodgrain shortage meant that a larger area needed to be cultivated to produce the earlier output of foodgrains for India. However, due to the Partition there was a serious shortage of raw cotton and raw jute as well because these were crops that were grown in East and West Pakistan. India could not overlook the requirement of these raw materials either. This led to competitive pressure on the available land. Industry could not, going forward, find it easy to acquire land. The government, too, had a disproportionate focus on agricultural development. The schemes of industrial development suffered as a result.

The new government in Delhi, therefore, developed a plan for the economic development of the country. The government proclaimed that it would promote both public and private entrepreneurship.

Meanwhile in early 1947, Gujarmal had set up a paints and varnish factory. This was a major step in the Indian market as the local manufacturing of paints and varnish was not well developed and most of the paint was imported. Shalimar Paints had established a paints factory in the early 1900s but there were not too many large factories till Independence.

Gujarmal had also increased the pace of development of his textile mill. However, he ran into a problem with getting his machines for the factory on time. Due to Partition, the deliveries were affected even though the order had been placed in early 1947. Half the machines had been delivered but without the other half, the textile mill could not be operational.

Along with the delayed delivery of machinery, there was another problem faced by Gujarmal. Partition had caused economic hardship all around and the average Indian was suffering. When going through financial pressures, people look at liquidating their investments. This was the case with the shareholders of the Modi textile mills. A large number of shares were offloaded in the market by many investors as they needed cash. This resulted in a drop of the share price by almost half. The face value of the share, when issued, was ₹5 and the aftermath of Partition saw the same share trading at ₹2.50. Gujarmal knew that if the share price kept dropping, then the morale of the remaining shareholders would fall too. Further, with the depressed morale, it would be difficult to find new investors. Thus, he instructed his team to buy shares of Modi Textiles from the open market. He bought enough shares to get the price of the share back to ₹5. He had to spend a large sum to buy back his own shares, but it brought in an air of hope and optimism in the market about the Modi textile mills. This was in contrast to many other businessmen who had allowed their businesses to be wound up due to investors selling off their shares. People were heard saying that if Gujarmal Modi himself was buying back shares it meant that he was confident about the business. Slowly, investors started coming back into the Modi textile mills.

Modinagar, by now, was a bustling town. Gujarmal did not belong to a royal family but he treated Modinagar as his personal riyasat. He ran it with total authority—almost like a benign authoritarian. The time spent in Patiala and observing Bhupinder Singh had rubbed off on his mannerisms. Though he still lived a simple life, his mannerisms were similar to that of a king.

Gujarmal needed to drive to Delhi often to meet with government officials. As the car reached the highway, Gujarmal would tap the driver on the shoulder and instruct him to slow down and drive at 60 km/hr. Gujarmal's car was a distinctive one and was easily identifiable. No car on the highway could overtake Gujarmal's car. Such was the power of the man that, no matter what speed he drove at, no one dared to overtake him on the highway. The unwritten rule laid down by Gujarmal was—'No one can cross my path and no one can come between my work and me.'

Gujarmal was particularly bothered by the delay in the delivery of the machines for his textile mill. By May 1948, when there was no news, Gujarmal decided to send his half-brother Kedarnath to the UK to check on the status of the machinery. Kedarnath was sure that the Indian high commission and the high commissioner would help him, but he had not bargained for government apathy. In the new independent India, businessmen were looked upon with scepticism and suspicion. People in the high commission did not know of either Kedarnath or the Modi textile mills and, thus, took no notice of this matter. He was disappointed but could not do much.

While he was in London, Kedarnath saw an advertisement for an industrial fair. He decided to go there in the hope of meeting some more businessmen and machinery suppliers. The press was covering the industrial fair and there were many journalists present on site. Kedarnath sensed an opportunity and spoke to a few press people. He told them that it seemed to him that industries in Britain were not doing well as orders placed two years ago were still undelivered. He further told them that due to British companies not being able to meet their obligations, the Modi textile mill had taken a decision to cancel the order and place an order in America. Kedarnath said that this decision of theirs would make the British machinery-makers lose an order worth ₹1 crore.*

The next day, Kedarnath's interview was highlighted in one of the major newspapers. This caused a furore in the UK. The industries minister of the UK was not happy that a native Indian was running down British companies. Even though they had left India, the attitude of the British was still that of looking down on all things Indian. The British bureaucrats spoke with their Indian counterparts and gave a statement that Kedarnath was just an average trader and did not have the capacity to pay for the machines ordered. This statement, in turn, enraged Kedarnath. He called the journalists and showed them the letters of credit of various banks, thus, proving his ability to pay for the machines worth ₹1 crore. Meanwhile the high commission had called up India and asked for more details on Kedarnath and his brother Gujarmal. They were surprised at the information received from India. They realized that Kedarnath

---

* In 1945, it was approximately GBP 75,000 at the prevailing exchange rate (INR 13.5 to 1 GBP)

was part of a successful family that had a large business group in India along with many factories. They were also surprised to know that there was a town named in honour of Kedarnath's brother. The Indian high commissioner quickly sent the details to the office of the industries minister of the UK.

Having realized their mistake in treating Kedarnath as an ordinary trader, both the high commission and the British government now wanted to help him get the machines on time. However, it was the factories in the UK that were unable to commit to a date of delivery. Kedarnath had no choice but to cancel the orders and go to the US, where he placed the order.

All the articles about the Modi family and the British government had an undesirable fallout in India. These articles brought Gujarmal under the spotlight which, in independent India, was unwelcome. The Indian government, after 1947, viewed industrialists with scepticism. The new government believed that many businessmen had amassed great wealth during the years of the Second World War. To detect instances of tax evasion, the government had set up an inquiry board. The board was equipped with great powers—their decision could not be appealed, and no lawyer could petition them. The business world was in a tizzy. Gujarmal, thanks to the spotlight thrown in the UK on the Modi family, also came to the notice of the board. This was a problem that Gujarmal could have done without. He was already battling the volatile share market and raising the required capital for his mill. He was also worried about importing the machines on time. Now he had to spend time with the board and wade through all the paperwork. Some well-wishers advised him to wind up the textile mill project. However, Gujarmal believed that lost money could be earned back easily but if he lost the trust of the public by shutting down the textile mill project, he would not be able to earn that trust back again for a long time. He, therefore, decided to go ahead with the project. Meanwhile, in 1948, the Modi Hosiery Factory and the Modi Tent Factory were started. This was also the year the Modi High School was extended to become the Modi Science and Commerce College.

Meanwhile, with the new machines ordered from the US, the work on the Modi textile mill was progressing well. Once finished and operational, the mill would need a minimum of 2,000 workers. As the workers normally came with their families, this meant that Modinagar would see an influx of at least 4,000–6,000 new residents. Gujarmal wanted to set up a new colony for the new workers. He also saw that Partition had created many refugees who needed to be rehabilitated. He decided to approach the Uttar Pradesh government with a proposal.

Gujarmal sought a meeting with Govind Ballabh Pant, the chief minister of the state. 'Sir, I want to develop a colony for the refugees,' he told the CM. 'I will train and provide them work in my new textile mill as well. For those who want to do something else, I will help them set up small-scale industries.'

'That is a good thought,' the CM was reported to have said and wanted to know how the government could help in this noble initiative.

'I need a loan from the government to set up this colony,' replied Gujarmal. He also promised that he would return the money with interest to the government. 'All the facilities that are available to my workers in Modinagar will be available to the refugees as well,' promised Gujarmal. The CM was happy at this proposal as the refugee problem was indeed a big one. A loan of ₹30 lakh was sanctioned by the UP government.

In June 1949, the Modi textile mill was finally ready. By this time, Dayawati and Gujarmal had been blessed with another child—a son. The name of this factory was Modi Spinning and Weaving Mills and that of their fourth son was Bhupendra Kumar. The mill was inaugurated by Chief Minister Govind Ballabh Pant. He also laid the foundation stone for the new colony for the refugees. The colony was named Govindpuri in honour of the chief minister.

Gujarmal had fifteen industries by now, was not yet fifty years old and was known in the business community as a self-made man despite his heritage. He was, however, getting a little frustrated at the socialistic bent of the government and the policies. He did not shy away from articulating his thoughts. In March 1949, he was invited to address the gathering of the All India Manufacturers Organisation in Delhi. Prime Minister Jawaharlal Nehru was the chief guest of the gathering. In his address, Gujarmal lamented the fact while the country had political freedom, it would mean very little unless there was economic freedom as well. At another platform, the North Western Regional Chamber of Commerce, Gujarmal said: 'If the people of the country are poor and hungry then the country cannot have either economic stability or a political one.' Gujarmal strongly believed that industrialization was the way to economic success.

A staunch believer in entrepreneurship, Gujarmal continued with the expansion of his businesses. In 1950, his sixteenth business was inaugurated by the minister of industries of Uttar Pradesh. This was a factory that produced top-quality lanterns. A large part of India in 1950 was still not electrified and the entire country had an installed capacity of only 1713 MW and the per capita consumption of electricity was 15 kWh. People needed other sources of light, especially at night. Lanterns that used oil to light a wick were the most popular source of light for most people. However, the good ones came from Germany and were expensive. The Modi Lantern Factory produced lanterns of quality that were comparable with the German ones. When inaugurated, the lantern factory could produce 5,000 lanterns per day. Due to the demand, the factory had to work at full capacity.

***

In all the expansions of the business and the time spent on business matters, there were two passions of Gujarmal that he found time for every day. One was keeping fit and healthy, and the other was playing the game of bridge. Gujarmal prided himself on his fitness levels as he made sure that he went for long brisk walks and then exercised. The other love of his—a game of bridge—was shared with his wife. Dayawati and he would play their daily games of bridge without fail.

Given his regimented lifestyle and focus on fitness, Gujarmal could not even think that he may have had any medical problems. Therefore, it came as a rude shock to him to find out that he may not have been as fit as he thought himself to be. In 1951, he went to a tea party in Meerut where one of the reputed doctors of the city was also present. After the tea party was over, Dr Karauli offered to drop Gujarmal home. As they climbed down the stairs, the doctor found Gujarmal breathing heavily. He advised Gujarmal to get a medical check-up done with a focus on the heart. Though Gujarmal did not take the advice seriously, the good doctor prevailed upon him and offered to fix an appointment with a cardiologist in Delhi.

'Dayawati, look at this doctor! He says that I need a heart check-up,' said Gujarmal as he entered his house and met his wife. He took off his jacket and handed it to Dayawati so that she could hang it in the cupboard. 'Look at me, do you believe my heart needs any checking?' he continued as he took off his cap and put it on the side table.

Dayawati kept quiet for a while. She was worried at the doctor's advice but wanted to keep calm. 'If the doctor wants you to have a check-up, how can it be harmful anyway?' she said softly as she fluffed up the cushion on the chair so that her husband could sit comfortably. 'You should go to Delhi and I can come with you.'

'Okay, okay, I will go for my check-up,' said Gujarmal as he lowered himself on to the chair. 'But remember, I am doing this only for you.' Dayawati smiled fondly at her husband.

The medical tests revealed that there were two leaking valves in Gujarmal's heart. This is a medical problem in which the valve in the heart does not close fully and allows some blood to flow backward into the left part of the heart. If left untreated, a leaky valve could lead to heart failure in the patient. Gujarmal could not believe that he had this medical condition. 'But I do not feel any pain nor any discomfort, doctor sahib,' he told the doctor. The cardiologist explained to Gujarmal that the medical equipment and tests did not lie. He also advised Gujarmal to restrict his vigorous walks and to avoid climbing steps.

Gujarmal did not like this at all. He did not want to lead a lazy life. He wanted to prove the doctor wrong. He decided to go for a pilgrimage to Badrinath. When some of his friends cautioned him, Gujarmal said, 'It is said in our scriptures that if you die while on a pilgrimage, you attain mukti or nirvana.' The logic in his mind was that if he came back alive and healthy, it would prove the doctor wrong; if he died while on the pilgrimage, he would attain nirvana. No one could dissuade Gujarmal from taking the trip. Even the fact that Dayawati and he had been blessed with their fifth son—Umesh Kumar—in early 1951 could not come in the way of his decision to travel.

Dayawati tried her best to change her husband's mind but in vain. She then decided to accompany her husband. As she was still breastfeeding the baby, Umesh Kumar was also part of the group. She had thought that Gujarmal would not want his wife and newborn son to go through the difficult pilgrimage and would change his own plans. But Gujarmal happily agreed to take his wife and youngest son along. He also asked his parents if they too wanted to come along with the group. Multanimal and his wife, though old, also decided to undertake the pilgrimage. Going on a tirth yatra or pilgrimage is important to Hindus. The Char Dham Yatra, or the pilgrimage to the four holiest shrines, is at the top of all pilgrimages. Badrinath is one of the char dham, the other three being Yamunotri, Gangotri and Kedarnath. Hindus believe that a pilgrimage to one of the these four dhams is a must in order to get salvation.

The Modi family group embarked upon the pilgrimage. It was not easy as the terrain was mountainous and the weather cold. However, the group persevered and reached Badrinath. A small havan ceremony was also done by the group. The pundits at the temple suggested a shraadh ceremony (prayer for the ancestors) be done by Multanimal. It was very cold, and the men had to sit bare-chested for the ceremony for a couple of hours in front of the priest. While Gujarmal did not suffer much, his father caught pneumonia. He had to be rushed to Haridwar for better care. Gujarmal spent over two months looking after his father. He was happy and relieved that despite his heart condition he had weathered the harsh conditions.

***

However, later in the same year, Gujarmal had to weather another storm in the business. In November 1951, Gujarmal was to go to Madras to address the Export Advisory Committee. Before he could leave, he was informed by Kedarnath that the Delhi Police had accused and framed charges against the Modis alleging that they had embezzled several thousand railway consignments worth several lakhs and that it had been done in collusion with the railway officials. Shocking as this news was, Gujarmal had no choice but to wait while simultaneously finding out the truth of the matter.

Gujarmal found out that the genesis of the matter was actually a heated argument between a movement officer of Modi Mills and the claims inspector of the railways. On a routine inspection, the claims inspector had got into a verbal fight with the movement officer of Modi Mills. The Inspection Raj of the new India had already started and inspectors could arrive at the factory and depots at any time to 'inspect' the premises. The underlying theme in all the inspections was that the industrialists were doing something wrong and hiding it from the government. The railway inspection officer had implied that Modi factories were involved in some unethical work, which had upset the movement officer. Heated words were exchanged, and the government officer felt insulted and aggrieved. In the newly independent India, government officers were held in high esteem while the people who worked for the lalas or seths were disregarded. The railway inspector wanted to teach the Modi employee and the Modi Group a lesson. He spoke to his brother-in-law, who worked in the police department. The brother-in-law told the inspector that if a complaint against the Modis were made, the government would be sure to investigate the matter because the new government was not very sympathetic to industrialists and capitalists in general.

The inspector made a whistle-blower complaint and addressed it to the prime minister's office. The complaint alleged that during the days of Partition, Gujarmal Modi had misappropriated consignments worth several lakhs of rupees. It was further claimed that this was carried out with the active support of some rogue railway officers. Since the matter concerned the railways, the prime minister's office forwarded the letter to the railways minister, who immediately ordered an investigation.

The case was given to the Special Police Establishment, who started a detailed inquiry by speaking with many employees of the Modi Group. Some simple people were threatened and cajoled by the investigating officers to implicate their seniors. Most of the employees were able to withstand the pressure. The investigating officers realized that Gujarmal Modi had enormous goodwill in the area. Thus, when the matter was to be taken to court, the investigating officers requested that instead of a local judge, a judge from Madhya Pradesh be brought in. It was said that since the accused was an influential industrialist of the area, it was feared that he might try to influence the local justices. The government was ready to spend a huge amount to fight this case.

The matter, as it transpired later, was actually a simple one. During Partition, due to the riots and killings, the railway network was disrupted and trains were unable to ply normally.

To avoid congestion on the route, the railway officers in Delhi had detained a large number of railway wagons carrying coal to areas of Western Punjab. The Western Punjab area was particularly affected as it was close to the borders of Pakistan. As the railways did not have enough sidings to hold these wagons, some industrialists in the area were requested to take some of these wagons to their private sidings. Thus, there were wagons dispatched to Modinagar as well. However, due to the overall confusion and chaos, many wagons carrying consignments of Modi factories were dispatched to other destinations in other parts of India. The Modi Group had informed the railways about this and had been in the process of sorting out the matter. Before the matter could be settled, the inspector had sent off the letter and an investigation had been initiated.

Gujarmal was perturbed about this investigation. He knew that if the matter came to court, there would be many problems. Primary among them would be the fact that any matter in court could take up to ten years for a firm verdict, and these years would be enough to ruin the reputation of the business and, therefore, the business itself. The next problem was that Gujarmal was sure that, given the socialist dispensation of the government, no court would rule in favour of a capitalist as the judges would be accused of being bribed. He tapped his political contacts and met with the minister for home affairs and the railway minister. He requested them to proceed with a court case only after a thorough investigation. However, he was told that, given the prevailing environment and the constant public gaze, the case could not be withdrawn.

When the matter could not be sorted out at the state level, Gujarmal took the matter to the Centre. Given the stature of Gujarmal Modi, the matter was discussed in the Union cabinet. Opinions of the advocate general, the attorney general and the law minister were sought. Simultaneously, the investigating agencies came back with their reports. Based on all this, the government finally concluded that the case against the Modis was a false and motivated one and that no prosecution be initiated in this.

Gujarmal heaved a sigh of relief, but the matter was symptomatic of the changed environment in India. The average Indian looked upon a businessman with suspicion. Partition had caused immense economic hardship across the board. The rich businessmen, though affected by the hardship, were able to weather it better due to their circumstances. The government, too, decidedly took on a socialist direction. Carrying on a business is not an easy task under any circumstances, but in the new India, it became even more difficult. What most industrialists found difficult to handle was the scorn heaped on to them by the average Indian. Any display of wealth was frowned upon as it was felt that the riches had been earned at the cost of the average Indian.

However, Gujarmal and other industrialists persevered. An interaction between Gujarmal and Pandit Nehru gave an insight into the mind of the government and the minds of the industrialists. Pandit Nehru had gone to Modinagar to give a speech about the abolition of the zamindari system, which had been in vogue for centuries in India. During the Mughal rule, the zamindars belonged to the nobility and formed the ruling class. Emperor Akbar had granted them mansabs and their ancestral domains were called jagirs. The word mansab is of Arabic origin and means rank or position. The zamindars did not own the land under the Mughals but were mansabdaars. When the British ruled India, they changed the system and gave ownership to the zamindars. They even bestowed titles like raja, nawab, etc., to the larger zamindars. The abolition of the zamindari system was one of the first major agrarian reforms of the Indian government after 1947.

Modinagar was decked up to welcome the prime minister. In spite of the rain, hundreds of men, women and children had gathered in the large grounds of Modi College to listen to Nehru's speech. After the speech, Gujarmal invited the prime minister to his home for a cup of tea and refreshments. The district congress committee officers objected to this. However, Gujarmal reminded them that he had invited Nehru for tea at home earlier, before he was the prime minister. Gujarmal said he saw no reason why the invitation could not be extended again. Nehru was reported to have said that if the invitation was for Jawaharlal, he would gladly accept. However, if the invitation was for the prime minister of the country, then he would have to respectfully decline.

It was decided that Gujarmal and Nehru would have tea together in a guest house in Muradnagar. This would be away from the large crowd that had gathered in Modinagar. Muradnagar was a short distance away from Modinagar and the guest house was situated on the banks of the Ganga Canal. The setting was informal and homely.

Nehru and Gujarmal sat on the verandah of the guest house. A simple tea and some snacks were served to them. Surrounded by greenery, the sounds of birds in the background put both men in a relaxed frame of mind.

'I am surprised by the reception given to me by industrialists and businessmen,' Nehru was reported to have said as he held a cup of tea in his hands and looked into the distance towards the gently flowing water of the canal. 'All of you know my party's philosophy but all of you seem to be welcoming me with open arms.'

'I know, sir, that you believe that socialism is the way to take India forward,' said Gujarmal as he, too, looked out in the distance. 'I know that many businesses may be nationalized in the coming years. But I also know that people like me are important in the economic development of our country. Maybe we want to tell you about our philosophy.' Gujarmal smiled as he put his cup down on the side table.

'You may be right, Gujarmal,' said Nehru. 'But I still do not understand why people, including people like you, want to shower me with so much attention.'

'Sir, you cannot claim to have fought big battles nor can you claim to be the most learned person in the entire country. But common people are still prepared to brave the heat, dust and rain to wait for hours to see you. I am sure that it is because of your past karmas,' said Gujarmal with his characteristic candour.

Nehru laughed loudly and poured himself another cup of tea. 'So, tell me now, Gujarmal, why are you so successful as an industrialist?' asked Nehru.

'Just like you are getting the benefit of your past karmas, I am sure that I must have also done some good deeds in my previous birth,' said Gujarmal quietly. 'I am not even a high-school pass but even then God has always fulfilled my wishes and made me a successful industrialist.' He paused. 'And let me remind you, sir, that people like me are the ones who provide employment to millions of people around the country. If we grow, our employees also grow. Only an economically strong India can take care of her people,' added Gujarmal as a last measure, looking intently at his guest.

'I have had a wonderful afternoon, Gujarmal. Let us keep it this way and agree to disagree,' said Nehru, smiling.

# 12

# *Adversity Is a Good Teacher*

THE year 1952 brought along with it more problems for Gujarmal. The frost had destroyed the sugarcane crop that year, which negatively affected the sugar mill. In the same year, the mill owners had produced large quantities of groundnut oil. By the months of March and April, when the groundnut crop was ready, the speculator-traders had entered the market. The speculators sold large quantities of groundnut oil and drove down the prices. The market slumped.

Gujarmal was now fifty years old but age had not slowed him down in any manner. He was travelling upcountry around this time. He had gone to Nasik for business purposes. When he reached Bombay from Nasik, he heard from Modinagar that the matter was serious as the oil mill was sitting on large stocks but the price in the market was falling steeply. He was also told that the book profit of over ₹8 lakh accrued on the basis of the stock in the inventory had already been wiped off. The price of oil had crashed from ₹70 per mann to less than ₹40 per mann.

Gujarmal cut short his visit to Bombay and rushed back to Modinagar. By the time he returned, the accrued profit of ₹8 lakh had turned into a notional loss of ₹20 lakh. The people in the mill were in a tizzy as they saw the price of oil fall almost every hour. Further, the crash in groundnut oil prices had spread to other commodities as well. Prices of commodities like oil, gold, silver and even cotton started falling sharply. The contagion was spreading fast as a bearish sentiment took hold of the market. As the prices fell, the share prices of companies producing and trading in these commodities also fell. As the share prices fell, the banks started getting worried because they had lent money to these companies. The banks were in danger of these loans turning into NPAs. The matter was getting serious.

Even Modi Oil Mills came under financial pressure. While a large number of employees readily took a salary cut to help the company, there were others who preferred to leave the company. Some senior managers left the company as they were not sure how long the slump would last. The directors of Modi Oil Mills were worried, and a meeting of the board was called. Some of the directors on the board were speculator-traders themselves. They were of the view that all stock of oil with Modi Oil Mills be sold to cut the losses as they were sure that the prices would fall further. Further, they suggested to Gujarmal that the funds with Modi Oil Mills be used to speculate in the commodity market by betting on gold and silver.

Gujarmal cut short these suggestions firmly and advised the board to hold on. He was sure that the market could not stay depressed for long and anyone who had the financial capacity to hold on would benefit in the long run. He was also wary of trading in gold and silver as he held no stocks of these commodities. The board meeting went on for a few hours and Gujarmal was at his persuasive best. Finally, the board gave permission to the management to refrain from panic-selling.

Gujarmal's foresight bore fruit. After a few days, the market turned, and the prices started going up again and the overall loss was contained to manageable levels. Gujarmal did not like accumulated losses in the business and did not want to carry them forward. Thus, he decided to sell off a plot of land he had bought on Najafgarh Road in Delhi to set up a vanaspati plant. He had paid ₹0.50 per square yard for the plot and in a short time the price had gone up to ₹6 per square yard. He sold this land at market price and also sold his oxygen gas plant he had set up a year ago.

The year 1952 was only the second time in his life that he had seen losses. The first time was in 1934 when the sugarcane crop had failed. At that time, his sugar mill was only a year old and the business was small. He had been able to sustain the losses. In less than two decades, Gujarmal had become a big industrialist and had created a personal brand equity. He had had a good run over the last decade and did not have to test his goodwill in the market. This year gave him an opportunity to step back and take a look at his business and relationships. He did not like what he saw in its entirety.

Success has many fathers while failure has none—this statement was manifested during this year. The problem of Modi Oil Mills was known to everyone and the fact that Gujarmal could incur heavy losses was also widely known. Gujarmal was a proud man and did not ask any of his relatives for financial help at this time. However, he was mindful of the sarcastic comments and loose talk behind his back by people whom he thought were close to him. He realized that not everyone had been happy at his success.

The other insight he gained from this period was that the business needed a reserve fund. The markets would continue to be volatile, and only those businesses which could ride out the volatility due to financial security would emerge as winners. If he had had a reserve fund that could have been used to ride out the oil price slump, Gujarmal was sure that he would not have had to sell off the prized piece of land in Delhi nor his oxygen gas plant.

Gujarmal also learnt another hard lesson. He had always prided himself on creating a loyal workforce. Modinagar was a town for workers, where they were given most facilities by the company. Most employees were given either a two-bedroom or three-bedroom house to live in, with all the amenities provided. Further, Dayawati and Gujarmal themselves took personal interest in the welfare of the workers. The Modi family was present for the workers in their time of need. Therefore, he was shocked to see some workers and managers leave the company when the business was going through a rough patch. He learnt the bitter lesson that he could not bank on the loyalty of his employees. The year 1952 turned out to be instructive for Gujarmal and the lessons he learnt stayed with him throughout his later years.

# 13

# *The Family Man*

GUJARMAL had always been a practising Hindu. He was a strict vegetarian and a teetotaller. Every morning, after his walk, exercise and bath, he would spend time praying and meditating. Every evening there was an hour of bhajans and readings from the Ramayana at home. Everyone was expected to sit together for this hour. The children, too, were not exempted from this evening hour of prayers and devotional songs.

In the years since 1932, when he had left Patiala to go to Begumabad to set up his dream industrial town, he had had no time to visit the various holy shrines in India, apart from Badrinath. Dayawati and he, however, did take personal interest in building temples in Modinagar. But Gujarmal had a deep desire to visit Gangotri in the Himalayas.

After the turbulent 1952 was over, the next year began on a positive note. The losses of the previous year were recouped, and business was back on track. Gujarmal decided it was a good time to go on a pilgrimage to Gangotri. Dayawati and a couple of other people formed part of the small group.

Going for these pilgrimages in the mountains was an arduous task in the middle of the twentieth century. There were no pucca roads that the travellers could take. Along with the absence of roads, there were no bridges and the travellers had to, perforce, cross the many streams and rivulets on foot. The kuccha roads themselves were very narrow and ran along the edge of the mountains with deep falls on the side. As if to compensate for all the hardship, nature provided the travellers, who were brave enough to take these routes, a breathtaking landscape. The majesty of the mountains and the beauty of the River Ganga was on full display.

While there was no road infrastructure on these paths, there were government guest houses along the way. Almost every ten or fifteen kilometres saw one dak bungalow, as the guest houses were called. These were lodges with one or two rooms and a kitchen. The facilities were very basic and not luxurious by any standards. There were also private dharamshalas—dormitories—along the way, but these were not very clean.

The pilgrims were undeterred by these hardships, and people of all ages undertook this yatra. It was common to see old men and women walking slowly with a bundle of their belongings on their heads. Gujarmal and his group did not have to carry any stuff on their heads. They had porters and mules to carry their belongings. Warm clothes were needed as it was biting cold up in the mountains. When they reached Gangotri, the Modi group stayed in a private bungalow of a businessman.

The area around Gangotri, the source of River Ganga, was not inhabited by villagers. There were only a couple of huts where a group of four or five sadhus lived. Gujarmal went to these huts after taking a bath in the bone-chilling waters of the river. He found that there was one sadhu who was in a tiny hut, not more than five feet in height. The entrance to the hut was so low that people had to crawl almost supine to enter. There was no space for more than three people inside. In this hut the sadhu sat alone on a wooden platform. In the cold he sat nude, unmindful of the weather. Though his eyes were open, he stared into the distance without blinking. The sadhu was in deep meditation.

As he went inside the hut, Gujarmal felt a strange connection with this sadhu. He spent hours at the sadhu's feet and felt his worries slowly leave him. He wanted to stay there at night but was told that no one could spend the night in the hut. He was advised to go back to the guest house. But he found himself unable to leave the place. He spent the night outside the hut and as soon as it was morning, he went back inside to see the sadhu. Gujarmal told the sadhu that he felt a strange connection with him and wanted him as his guru. The sadhu, through a gesture, indicated that he could not take on Gujarmal as a disciple. But Gujarmal could not take no for an answer. The night that he had spent outside the hut had strengthened his resolve that there was indeed a strange connection between them.

Gujarmal was relentless when it came to pursuing his business goals. Getting the sadhu to be his guru became his personal goal. He decided that he would not leave Gangotri till the sadhu agreed to give him guru-diksha. Diksha is the giving of a mantra or an initiation by a guru, usually in a one-on-one ceremony. He decided that Dayawati and the rest of the group would go back to Modinagar, and he would wait in attendance in Gangotri.

Gujarmal would spend the day in the hut and talk to the sadhu. He told the sadhu that he had been searching for a guru for thirty years. Gujarmal further said that his heart told him that he had found the guru here. His persistent pursuit bore fruit. The sadhu relented and agreed to give Gujarmal guru-diksha. Gujarmal was ecstatic and organized a large bhandara (public food offering). Amid the chants of vedic mantras, Gujarmal was initiated as a disciple of the guru. He now wanted to stay back in the service of his guru. However, his guru instructed him to go back as he had a responsibility towards his family—his daughters had to be married and his sons taken care of, besides the fact that his wife also needed looking after. Gujarmal could not go against his guru's wishes and returned. But he returned with joy in his heart as he felt that he had achieved a lifelong ambition of finding the right guru.

Gujarmal went back to Gangotri a year later and spent a few days with his guru. He told his friends that if it were left to him, he would spend the rest of his life in the service of his guru. But once again, the sadhu reminded his disciple that as an industrialist he was serving people because he was providing livelihood to them. The sadhu said that Gujarmal was also serving the nation by building factories and mills, thus taking India on a path of success. The sadhu's words resonated with Gujarmal and he saw the work he was doing in a new light. He promised that he would continue the work of consolidating and expanding his business ventures.

Two years after his guru-diksha, Gujarmal travelled with his family to Prayagraj to take a dip in the confluence of the three rivers. This time he took almost a month off and also visited other religious places of Gaya, Varanasi, Ayodhya and Chitrakoot. After he had immersed himself in work for almost two decades, he took this time to immerse himself in bhajans, kirtans, spiritual and religious discourses. The simple living, many times in camps, brought him in touch with the basic pleasures of life.

But Gujarmal had not forgotten the words of his guru and had continued to set up new businesses. He had been forced to sell his oxygen plant to fund the losses due to the slump in groundnut oil prices. In 1954, he set up a new oxygen plant. He also bought a tube well company that was owned by a British firm. The decade of 1946–56 was a good one for Indians who wanted to buy firms owned by Britishers. The British were not very confident of their businesses doing well after India became independent. They were looking to sell off their businesses, sometimes at a throwaway price. Gujarmal saw the tube well company as one such opportunity. The asking price was ₹12 lakh but Gujarmal was able to buy the entire company, along with the assets, for only ₹5 lakh. He brought that company to Modinagar and named it Associated Tubewell Company. By this time, his eldest daughter had been married to Jayanti Prasad Agarwal. Gujarmal entrusted the running of this company to his son-in-law. Gujarmal preferred bringing family members into the business as he believed that he could trust them. He had already brought in his half-brothers and given them charge of various factories. Now it was the turn of the next generation.

***

His sons were in boarding school. Gujarmal, himself, had not cleared high school and it was a source of regret for him. He was, therefore, determined that his sons would complete their education from the best institutes. Modinagar had a good high school. Gujarmal had ensured that talented teachers came to teach at Modi High School. All his sons went to the local school for their primary studies. Gujarmal had instructed the school not to give any special treatment to his sons. But it was difficult for teachers and fellow students to overlook the fact that these were the children of the founder of their town. There was a certain deference that crept in and Gujarmal was uncomfortable with it. Further, the schools in Modinagar were Hindi-medium. Gujarmal wanted his sons to be fluent and conversant in English.

Not only did he want his sons to study well, Gujarmal, with his focus on physical fitness, also wanted all his sons to go to a school where they would get the right opportunities to play sports on a larger scale. He knew that the local schools in Modinagar could not offer him and his sons this aspect of all-round development. Further, he realized the importance of a 'network'. The business families had their own network but Gujarmal realized that a network developed with fellow students in a good school lasts a lifetime. He knew that he had to send his sons to a good boarding school.

He discussed the matter with Dayawati and got her agreement to send the boys away from home. He had discussed the options for boarding schools with other Marwari families. He had also visited some schools to find out, first-hand, more about the schools and their philosophies. Based on his discussions and the general perceptions of the various schools, the shortlist was composed of three schools—Doon School, Mayo College and Scindia School.

Gujarmal dismissed Doon School outright. 'I don't want my sons to become bada sahibs and focus on smoking and drinking,' he told Dayawati contemptuously. 'The school is very anglicized and my sons will forget about their Indian culture and even Hindi if they go there.'

'And I don't want my sons to think of themselves as rajas and maharajas,' he explained the reason for rejecting Mayo College from his list.

That left Scindia School. This school was the first choice for well-off Marwari families who believed that the school and its environment provided the right balance of studies and all-round development. 'I found that the school has a focus on our Indian culture and values,' Gujarmal told Dayawati upon his return from a visit to the school. 'English and Hindi, both languages are taught to the children. Every evening all the boys have to wear kurta-pyjama and go for an hour of bhajans. I saw that all food was served in thalis,' Gujarmal said with satisfaction.

The Scindia School was indeed focused on Indian values and culture but gave its students a global outlook as well. There was ample scope for outdoor activities too. For over 500 boys, the school had forty-four fields for different sports. What Gujarmal liked most about the school was that the focus was on all-round personality development.

In the 1950s, almost half of the boys passing out of Scindia School joined the armed forces. Though it was not a military school, the discipline was that of an army school. This was the factor that tipped the balance for Gujarmal. He was focused on discipline too and found the school's philosophy matching his own. 'After they finish school, I will send each of my sons to do engineering. They will all be engineers,' he told Dayawati confidently.

The sons, as they reached the right age, were sent to Scindia School. The children would come home for holidays and the older ones would be taken to spend time at the office. In the summer holidays, however, all the children were packed off to the family home in Mussoorie—a hill station in Uttar Pradesh (present day Uttarakhand). Two teachers—one male and one female—from the local Modi school would be sent along with the children as chaperons.

The children on vacation were not exempt from Gujarmal's brand of discipline. Every child would be given his/her own holiday allowance for the two months they would spend in Mussoorie. Gujarmal's rule was that the allowance had to last the entire holiday period. The day some child's allowance finished—and the hawk-eyed teachers monitored the amounts—they had to go back to Modinagar. It was Gujarmal's way of teaching his children to live within the means they had. 'If you have ten rupees, make sure that you live your life for two months within this amount,' was the message he gave the children each year as he waved them off to Mussoorie.

Though a warm-hearted and generous person, Gujarmal lived his life with military precision. And he wanted his children to follow his example. The children also learnt quickly not to cross the invisible line between respect and affection. Gujarmal did not believe in showing affection to his sons—with his daughters, he was a little more generous. The role of a father was clear in Gujarmal's mind—it was to pass on the knowledge that he had gathered to his sons so that they could carry on his legacy.

Dayawati was a tender person and more generous with her affection to all her children. However, there was a no-nonsense air about her and her children teased her saying that she had acquired it from her husband. Dayawati knew that her husband had strict rules about everything, and woe betide anyone who crossed him or any of his rules.

One rule was that when Gujarmal slept in the afternoon he could not be disturbed. Dayawati instructed all her children, and even the staff, to ensure that if they were driving back home, the car was parked a fair distance away so that the noise would not intrude on Gujarmal's sleep. The children, after parking the car, had to tip-toe around the house and whisper quietly to make sure that they did not wake their father.

When it came to the matter of discipline, Gujarmal did not differentiate between his own and his brother's sons. All of them had to follow the good-behaviour guidelines as laid down by him. All boys had been told to study engineering, and they did. Gujarmal instructed the next generation to live like the other boys in the hostel when they were in engineering colleges. 'You should be the last person in the entire college to get any special benefits. No one should know that you come from a wealthy household,' he thundered each time any of the boys gathered up the courage to ask for anything extra. The boys were all expected to live in the hostel and ride bicycles around town.

One of Gujarmal's nephews was studying engineering at the Thapar Institute of Engineering in Patiala. One of Gujarmal's half-brothers lived in Patiala and was the local guardian of Kedarnath's son. It was the nephew's misfortune that the day the exams results had been declared, his uncle had come to Patiala. As was his habit, Gujarmal landed up unannounced at his nephew's hostel. His half-brother Harmukh Modi, the local guardian of the boy, accompanied him. Gujarmal was enraged when he found that his nephew had failed to clear his exams.

'Show me your room. I want to go to your room,' Gujarmal ordered his nephew.

The nephew had no choice but to take his uncle to his room. Once there, Gujarmal started an inspection of the small hostel room. He went through the bookshelf, looked under the bed, and even opened a suitcase. When he looked under the pillow, Gujarmal snatched the book he saw there. It was a racy thriller with a picture of a semi-naked girl on the cover.

Gujarmal looked at his nephew with disgust and slapped him hard across the face. 'Now I understand the reason you failed. You are spending your time reading this disgusting stuff?' he thundered.

As the nephew tried to melt into the floor, Gujarmal turned to his half-brother and said, 'It is your fault. You were supposed to take care of this boy. And look what he's spending his time doing.'

It did not matter to Gujarmal that he was admonishing not his own son, but that of his brother. And the nephew also did not find it inappropriate that it was his uncle, and not his father, who was giving him a verbal hiding. The nephew swore to Gujarmal that he would study hard. In later years the nephew held his uncle squarely responsible for making it possible for him to clear his exams. 'I could not bear another day like that one,' the nephew said later.

***

The factories and businesses in Modinagar kept growing. After the success of the cotton cloth mill that was set up in 1948–49, Gujarmal now wanted to set up a silk mill. The silk mill was ready for inauguration in 1956 and Gujarmal requested the chief minister of the state to do the honours. Govind Ballabh

Pant readily agreed and came to Modinagar. As he arrived, a drizzle started. 'Oh, it is a good omen,' said many people. The drizzle, however, soon turned into a downpour, which lasted the entire night.

By the morning the entire town of Modinagar was under four feet of water. The new silk mill was a mess, as were all the other mills and factories. The machines were all under water and the rolls of finished cloth material were floating in the water. The rainwater had entered the storerooms. Dyes and colour pigments got mixed with the water, giving it a multi-coloured hue. In the sugar mill, the ready sugar—tonnes and tonnes of it—was washed away. The torrential rain all through the night had also washed away parts of the railway track. The roads were inundated, and no travel was possible. Modinagar became like an island, cut off from the rest of the world.

Luckily Modinagar also had some army presence as the Meerut Cantonment was only a few kilometres away. The military boats were pressed into service to distribute water, medicines and some food items to the marooned families. By the third day, the waters had receded, and the sun was back in the sky. The residents of Modinagar heaved a sigh of relief and started the work of cleaning up their houses, the factories, the roads, the shops and so on.

In the midst of the hectic cleaning process, a shout went up from people on the roads. 'The water is coming back! Watch out, the water is coming back!' cried the people. Women stopped their work and looked up at the sky. The sun was shining brightly and there was not even a speck of a rain cloud. Dismissing the cry as a hoax, the women went back to cleaning their houses. But soon enough, they could see the water swirling and coming back into their houses. Everyone was perplexed as they could not understand the reason for their town flooding.

Hectic enquiries revealed that this time the flooding was man-made. The rainfall had not only been torrential in Modinagar, but even the areas upstream, near the Himalayas, had seen heavy rains. As a result, the water level in the River Ganga had gone above the danger mark. Modinagar was near the Ganga Canal which passed through Muradnagar, and there was excess water in the canal as well. To protect the bigger towns like Bulandshahr from flooding, the authorities had opened the outlets of the Ganga Canal about 5 kilometres away from Modinagar. This released the pressure on the canal but flooded the area. There were some nullahs (drains) to catch the overflow of water, but the volume of water released from the canal proved too much for the nullahs to handle. The railway track had some underbridges but these were shallow, narrow and not designed to handle these large volumes of fast-flowing water.

For a while before the flooding, Gujarmal had been requesting the government for infrastructure development work, but the authorities had been dragging their feet. He took this calamity as an opportunity to push his request through. He invited the local government officers to see the plight of the residents. When the officers demurred, Gujarmal gave them a graphic description of the misery faced by the residents of Modinagar. 'And this is not even their fault. This is not even due to the rain gods,' he told the officers. 'All it requires is for the underbridges to be widened. Then, in future, even if there is flooding, at least the water will be able to flow freely and will not get accumulated in Modinagar,' he added. The officers agreed and the underbridges were ultimately widened.

The days of the flood brought into focus the seva-bhav of Gujarmal. When Modinagar was flooded and the residents marooned inside their own houses, they saw Gujarmal wading through the water, alongside the army and other officers of the city. Unmindful of his own health or stature, Gujarmal personally supervised the distribution of rations to the people who needed them. In those dark times, Gujarmal appeared as a shining beacon of hope to the residents of Modinagar.

Indeed Modinagar had lived up to its name in India as a model township. It was well planned and the 'owner' or founder of the town personally ensured that the residents were provided with the facilities for daily living. The medical dispensaries were staffed with trained doctors and most of the services were provided free of cost to the residents.

The residents of Modinagar were witness to yet another side of Gujarmal. They saw him as a doting and dutiful husband to Dayawati. The residents saw both Gujarmal and Dayawati each evening as they went about their evening walk together at the Krishna Ashram. People who saw Dayawati attending functions on behalf of her husband would not have believed that she was a simple, unsophisticated young girl of seventeen years when she married Gujarmal. It was his guidance that had enabled her to be a partner of equal standing to her husband. She was a mother of eleven children and managed her large household with as much precision as her husband managed his large business empire.

Gujarmal looked upon his wife as Goddess Lakshmi. He had confessed to some close friends that he had been ready to give up the material world before he married Dayawati. It was after she came into his life that his fortune had started changing for the better. Dayawati continued to be the primary source of support for her husband. She was the one that her children went to whenever they were in a quandary. Even though not educated in the formal system, Dayawati had a sharp and analytical mind. Gujarmal relied on her advice and she never failed him. It was a jugalbandi in which each partner complemented the other.

# 14

# *Navigating the Licence Raj Maze*

MODINAGAR had established a high school and a commerce college for the children of its workers, and by the mid-1950s, both the educational institutions had established a name for themselves. There were over 20,000 workers and their families living in Modinagar by now. Gujarmal's children and nephews and nieces had also grown up in Modinagar. They had studied in the educational institutes set up by Gujarmal. One of Gujarmal's nephews wanted to study biology in college. Since the college in Modinagar was only a commerce college, the nephew had to look for other institutes. The nearest degree college was in Meerut.

Meerut College had been established in 1892 and was one of the premier educational institutes of the country. Scholars came from across the country to study there. Gujarmal had included Meerut College in his philanthropic activities and had generously donated money from time to time. Now that his nephew wanted to enrol in biology honours in Meerut College, Gujarmal sent word to the principal of the college. He was sure that Madan Mohan, the principal, would help his nephew get admitted.

He was surprised, therefore, that his nephew came back dejected after his meeting with Madan Mohan. 'The principal told me that instead of sending a recommendation, why don't you ask your uncle to open a degree college in Modinagar?' said the nephew. Gujarmal could have taken umbrage at this rebuff but he chose to focus on the message.

'It is really a good idea,' he told his nephew. 'Modinagar does not have a degree college and many students are left without higher education.'

A decision to set up a degree college was taken and the foundation stone was laid in May 1957. Gujarmal was like a man possessed. He drove the workers hard to get the construction finished as early as possible. The work was completed in less than four months and in September 1957, the college was inaugurated. Starting with a hundred students, the college went on to educate thousands of students.

Almost a month after the inauguration of the college, Gujarmal lost his father—Multanimal Modi. The influence of his father in his life had been immense. He did not start any new work nor any new business without the blessings of his father. Multanimal had lived a full life and was over eighty years of age when he passed away. Gujarmal named the newly inaugurated college after his father and till date the college is known as Multanimal Modi College.

By the time the new college had been inaugurated, India had been independent for ten years. The political and social environment had changed since the days of the British Raj. The focus of the government was on the common man and the protection of workers from industrialists, who were looked upon with suspicion. The government also looked at the managing agency system with distrust.

The managing agency system was a corporate structure that had been prevalent in India since the early nineteenth century. Even the British used this structure to own and then run businesses in India. The managing agency system can, very loosely, be likened to the present structure of venture funds or private equity funds, with some differences. The managing agency structure allowed a few partners to set up and control a number of public or joint-stock companies even with very little shareholding of their own. Men with great entrepreneurial abilities and sound reputation were able to set up a managing agency and raise funds from the public. These funds were used to buy into a business or set up a new one. The management contract between the business and the agency allowed the managing partner to set the business goals and policies.

The managing agency system filled the gap that existed for entrepreneurs in India when it came to seeking funding. The capital markets were not well developed and the banks were not prepared to finance the long-term needs of the industry. At most, the banks could lend working capital for a short term to those who needed it. The managing agency system was, therefore, a good way to develop business ability and to put the limited finance available to the best use. As is with any other system, the managing agency system was also prone to misuse. The new government in India saw the managing agency system as a concentration of economic power in the hands of a few. The Indian Companies Act of 1956 brought in strict guidelines for the running of businesses. The act required public companies and their subsidiaries to get prior government approval for the appointment and remuneration of managerial personnel and their relatives and associates. Four categories of managerial personnel were defined under the act—managing agents, secretaries and treasurers, managing directors and managers.

The government, since Independence, had brought about several new laws and regulations. All these reflected the socialist thinking and welfare model of development. The new government, in its enthusiasm, overlooked the fact that a welfare model works when the government's coffers are full. India at independence was left struggling economically. A welfare and socialistic model that worked in the more developed and wealthier nations had no chance of being successful in a poor and hungry country.

Notwithstanding any of the voices to the contrary from industry and industrialists, the government enacted a series of acts. One of these was the Minimum Wages Act of 1948. This act took away the freedom of setting wages from business owners. It was the government that decided the wages to be paid. The Factories Act of the same year was yet another law enacted to protect workers by regulating the condition of labour in factories. It seemed to the industrialists that this law was rooted in the premise that all entrepreneurs were evil and exploitative while it was the government that was the saviour of the workers. With one stroke of the pen, the government gave an inordinate amount of power to the inspectors who could come to inspect the conditions within a factory at any time and without notice. This was the start of the Inspector Raj in which the inspectors could send factory owners to jail for as long as seven years for violating laws.

Along with the Inspector Raj, came the Licence Raj. In 1951, the Industries (Development and Regulation) Act was passed by the Parliament and this sounded the death knell for entrepreneurship in India. This act ruled that the central government would take control of industries and articles specified in the First Schedule. The thirty-eight industries ranged from machine tools and defence to telecommunications and electrical equipment; and 171 articles ranged from coal to fans to sewing machines and precious metals. This act also mandated that any new industry be set up only after taking a licence issued by the central government. Further, the act also gave the government the power to decide the location and the capacity of the industry. Even one unit produced in excess of the licenced number of units could lead to severe punishment of the owner.

Not content with these laws alone, the government went on a spree of nationalizing thriving businesses. In 1953, nine private airlines, including Tata Airlines (now called Air India), Kalinga Airlines, Bharat Airways, Deccan Airways, were taken over by the government and turned into two government airlines—Air India and Indian Airlines. And then, in 1955, the government took over the Imperial Bank of India and transformed it into the State Bank of India. The Imperial Bank was a private bank with only 20 per cent of its shareholding held by states. The year 1956 saw the Life Insurance Corporation Act being passed by the Parliament. This act nationalized 154 Indian and sixteen foreign insurance companies as well as seventy-five provident societies into the mammoth Life Insurance Corporation of India (LIC).

The enactment of all the new laws had a dampening effect on entrepreneurship in India. The entrepreneurs also grew increasingly apprehensive of the appropriation of power by the hands of government officers—junior to senior—and politicians. There were two instances that fuelled Gujarmal's apprehension.

The first was the matter of Modi Mills in Okhla, Delhi. In 1957, a big flour mill in Delhi called Ganesh Flour Mill caught fire and burnt down completely. The food minister suggested to Gujarmal that the Modis set up a flour mill in Delhi. This idea was liked by all and the team started planning the flour mill. Machinery for the flour mill was ordered from Czechoslovakia. Gujarmal started looking for a suitable piece of land in Delhi to set up the mill. Under the new industrial laws, Gujarmal had to take permission from the government and their help in identification of the land for the flour mill.

This was a new experience for Gujarmal. He had set up many factories and had needed permission from the local authorities. But the granularity of the permissions required to set up a simple flour mill left him exhausted. A piece of land in Okhla, Delhi was finally identified in 1958 and Gujarmal bought it. He was surprised and upset, therefore, that soon after he purchased the land, the government acquired it back from him under the pretext of the land being reserved for the cottage industry.

Gujarmal was livid, and he was not one to mince words. He spoke with the ministers and the government officers and told them that he had not imagined the senior people breaking their own word. Though that specific piece of land in Okhla was irretrievable, Gujarmal was able to get another piece of land to set up Modi Mills. The work on the mill took a year and it was finally inaugurated in May 1959. Modi Mill continues to be a landmark in the Okhla area even after sixty years.

The other matter that caused Gujarmal dissonance with the workings of the government concerned his cloth mills in Modinagar. Gujarmal had always had cordial relations with the worker community in Modinagar. He looked upon each worker as a member of his own family. The workers, too, were happy being part of the Modinagar community. The town was built for them and they could not complain about the facilities.

However, by the end of 1957, some workers had started complaining about the lack of bonuses. The floods in 1956 had damaged almost all the machines of the cloth mills. The insurance had enabled Gujarmal to recover some of the losses, but the mill was not running at its full capacity. Even though the productivity had come down, the workers continued to get their full wages. However, they were not given their annual bonus.

Some local politicians took advantage of this discontent and incited the workers to go on a strike. Gujarmal was surprised that his workers had chosen to lay down their tools instead of coming to speak with him. As was his habit, he preferred to wait and watch. The workers, seeing no reaction from Gujarmal, started taking out processions chanting slogans against the Modi family. The local police was called to prevent the situation from escalating. Gujarmal still made no overtures to the agitating workers. He was upset and had a sense of being betrayed by his own people.

The local political leaders then advised the workers to resort to some theatrical measures to get a response from the management. Under their supervision, one worker lay down in the middle of the road and a small group of workers surrounded him. The group started shouting and crying that the police had lathi-charged them and one of their co-workers had died. The rest of the workers, who did not know about the theatrical plan, were shocked and flocked to the site. Seeing one of their own lying on the ground with eyes closed and motionless, the larger group of workers got agitated. The police grew unwilling to take any action against the crowd for fear of being accused of harsh action.

The district magistrate of Meerut saved the situation. Gyan Prakash, the DM, reached the site of the agitation and spoke with some members of the protesting group. When he asked them about the sequence of events, he felt that the story was not adding up. Further, he wanted the 'dead' worker to be taken to the hospital but the small group prevented him from doing so. Gyan Prakash was sure that he was not being told the truth.

He decided to do some theatrics of his own. While talking to the workers, he started moving towards the 'dead' worker on the ground. Though he kept talking to the small group, Gyan Prakash was watching the 'dead' worker from the corner of his eye. He saw the 'dead' man flinch a bit as Gyan Prakash's foot reached near his ear. The district magistrate understood that the man was pretending to be dead. He shouted out loudly and kicked the 'dead' man.

A collective gasp went around the gathered crowd. They thought that the DM had committed blasphemy. An even larger gasp went around the crowd when they saw the 'dead' worker get up after being kicked. The DM spoke to the 'dead' worker harshly, accused him of committing fraud and threatened to lock him up in jail. The worker started weeping and told the DM that it was all just a plan to get the other workers more agitated.

A large number of workers were not happy at the course these events were taking and wanted to call off their strike. But the political leaders were able to incite the worker union leaders and get them to continue the strike. By now the local administration had enforced prohibitory orders in the area under Section 144 of the Indian Penal Code. The agitating workers could not gather in large numbers within the limits of Modinagar. They set up their protesting camp just outside the limits of the town.

Gujarmal, by now, wanted to take matters in his own hands. He was encouraged by the number of the workers who wanted to call off the strike. He wanted to speak to the union leaders but the local political leaders prevented him from going to the group. The pretext used was that Gujarmal could be harmed by the agitating workers.

Gujarmal listened to the advice but did not heed it. He, along with a small group of his officers, went to the area where the workers had set up camp. He spoke to the workers and cautioned them from listening to outsiders who had no stake in the welfare of the people in Modinagar. Gujarmal requested the agitating workers to come to him directly if they had any complaints. The workers of Modinagar had always looked upon Gujarmal as one of their elders. When they saw Gujarmal Modi standing before them and asking them to think of Modinagar, the factories and their own families, the workers realized their mistake. They heard Gujarmal say, 'We are a family. If you have any problems, you can come to me. We can sit together like families do and solve all our issues.' The workers were disarmed by Gujarmal's concern and care.

Gujarmal further disarmed the workers by announcing that going forward, every morning, any worker who came to the mandir would get ₹1. Further, he announced that one meal for the workers and their families would be provided by the company. The members of his senior management team were aghast at this. But such was the stature and fear of Gujarmal that no one could question him outright. Some did gather the courage to ask him if giving money and food to the workers would not encourage them to continue their strike.

'The workers are striking about getting more wages and a bonus. The company will take a decision based on what is best for the situation,' said Gujarmal. 'However, whatever the decision, I cannot let my workers starve. After all, I am sure that the strike will end one day and soon. I want my workers to come back to work healthy and work hard to make up for lost time. If I don't ensure that they get at least one square meal a day, how will they work once they come back?'

The focus on worker welfare was primary in the mind of Gujarmal. Philanthropy was one reason for sure, but there was a hard, practical reason behind the welfare activities as well. Every worker who was employed by any of the Modi factories was given a house on nominal rent. While the land and the house belonged to the company, a worker living in a house never did vacate it. After living in it for thirty or forty years, it practically became his.

Gujarmal, since the time he had set up his first factory, was certain that his workers would live in a pucca house. When he built the factories, a residential complex for the workers was an integral part of the plan. 'If my worker stays in a jhuggi-jhopdi, how will he remain healthy? How will he give his full commitment to the work if he worries about his family living in unhygienic conditions?' was the question Gujarmal asked every time he was questioned about his obsession with worker welfare.

Thus, even at the time of the worker strike, Gujarmal was thinking ahead—of the time when the workers would come back to work. Contrary to what people believed about workers continuing their strike due to getting ₹30 a month—₹1 per day if they went to the mandir—the strike wound down soon after Gujarmal's meeting with them. The workers started trickling back to work.

Both these matters—the Modi Flour Mills debacle and the agitation in Modinagar—left a bad taste in Gujarmal's mouth. He realized that, going forward, doing business was not going to be easy and that there were new factors that had to be taken into account. One such factor was that the authorities were now handling all workers with kid gloves, given the focus of the government. Gujarmal had to, thus, take the hard call of shutting down some factories due to the inability to take action against workers for undesirable behaviour. A case in point was the biscuit factory in Modinagar. It was found that a section of the workers had started indulging in eating biscuits being produced within the factory. Some workers had also started carrying bags filled with biscuits outside and then distributing them to workers in other factories. The officers of the biscuit factory were prevented by union leaders from taking action against the rogue workers. Seeing that the erring workers were getting away scot-free, some of the other workers also started indulging in undesirable behaviour. A decision was taken to close down the biscuit factory as the losses due to the workers taking away the product increased. At the same time, the oil mill was also shut down as it too had started generating losses due to falling productivity.

The hallmark of an entrepreneur is a high spirit of enterprise no matter the odds. Thus, despite the challenges being faced, Gujarmal set up a distillery and another oxygen plant in Modinagar in 1957.

# 15

# *Saat Samundar Paar*

BY 1960, Gujarmal was counted among the top ten wealthiest men in the country. His business group was also among the top ten in the country. The successful businesses were the ones that were either dealing in commodities or others that focused on institutional sales. His businesses that produced branded products were not as successful. In modern times, these are called B2B and B2C businesses.

B2Bs are businesses that sell products and services to other businesses; B2C businesses, on the other hand, sell products and services directly to customers. The systems that form the backbone of the two types of businesses, that is, communication strategy, sales process, transaction, pricing, etc., differ in complexity, scope and even cost.

One of the key differences is the purchasing process of goods and services in the two types of businesses. In a B2C business, the customer buys the product for personal consumption. There is greater emotional involvement in the decision-making process. The brand and the brand equity of the product also play an important part in the decision. The decision to buy, or not to buy, is not dictated by anyone. B2B, on the other hand, is about buying products which are not for personal use—products are bought for companies or institutions. The decision-making is more complex and group-, rather than individual-, driven. The decision-making groups could include team members from the technical, finance, operations and business departments. Further, the decision to make purchases needs approvals and the point of view or preference of the owner or leader of the business plays an important role.

In the middle of the twentieth century, most businesses in India were family-owned and family-managed. The professional businesses were less than 10 per cent of the total operational businesses. India was also a market driven by supply rather than demand. Due to the acts passed by the government, which controlled the type and amount of goods produced by entrepreneurs, the Indian economy had become one driven by scarcity. Thus, for goods like sugar, steel, chemicals and commoditized cloth, the supply was always less than the demand; the entrepreneurs had no difficulty selling their products.

Matters were different when it came to branded products in the B2C category. It was here that most Indian companies missed the opportunity to capture the minds of the customers. This was the case with Gujarmal's businesses as well. A case in point was the toilet soap business.

Gujarmal had set up his toilet soap factory with great interest. Instead of using beef tallow, his factory had produced toilet soaps using vanaspati. The problems in the soap business started during the Second World War. All fragrances added to the soap were imported as India did not produce these locally. As all imports were affected, the quality of the soap produced went down. The big companies manufacturing soaps were Levers and Tata. Levers, in particular, had a well-defined marketing strategy for their consumer products, including soaps. Large amounts of money were spent by them to build the brand equity of their soaps. Further, Levers had a whole portfolio of consumer products, and they had a deep and robust sales channel that ensured that the retail outlets stocked their products. The sales channels also supplied publicity materials like posters and other display items to reinforce brand equity.

For Gujarmal Modi, the toilet soap—Prefect—was only one product in this category of consumer products. Thus, the sales channel was rudimentary and depended largely on the personal relationships that the salespeople had with the retail store owners. Gujarmal could not spend even a fraction of the money that Levers spent on developing the brand of his soap. Slowly the retailers started reducing their orders as they said that they would prefer to stock products that customers asked for.

The problem that the Tata company presented for Modi's soap was a different one. The Tatas used the leverage of their other products to get retailers to stock their soap. Tata Chemicals produced bleaching powder, which was always in high demand. The company would supply bleaching powder to only those retailers who also ordered their soaps. The profit margin in bleaching powder was high enough to enable the retailers to sell their stock of soap even at a discount.

Thus, Gujarmal was slowly edged out of the market and he decided to shut down the toilet soap factory. The carbolic soap, used for washing clothes, was driven more by price than the brand, and it continued to be produced and sold.

***

Notwithstanding these setbacks, the reputation and stature of Gujarmal continued to grow. In 1960, the government had set up an engineering college in Kanpur. Gujarmal was invited to be part of the board of governors. In the same year, the government set up a development council for man-made silk. Gujarmal was invited to be part of the council by the government. Gujarmal also established a branch of the National Productivity Council in Meerut—the Western UP Productivity Council—and he was elected as the first president. The public offices of Gujarmal continued to multiply as he was nominated, again by the government, as a member of the Central Custom Excise Advisory Committee. The UP government set up a board of technical education and nominated Gujarmal as a member. The Reserve Bank of India nominated Gujarmal as a director to their northern India board.

Gujarmal's sixtieth birth anniversary was approaching in 1962. By now his older sons were helping him in the business. His brother Kedarnath was his able assistant. There was almost a twenty-year age gap between the two brothers, and Kedarnath was happy to stay in the shadows of his older brother. The two had established a working relationship and pattern. Gujarmal was the visionary and the public face of the Modi Group; Kedarnath was the implementer of the vision. In modern terms, the two could be likened to CEO and COO.

Kedarnath understood his older brother very well. He also understood Gujarmal's attitude towards discipline and total loyalty. Kedarnath made sure that he did not give his brother any reason to question his obedience.

It was Gujarmal's youngest son Umesh Kumar's first day at work after having passed from Banaras Hindu University (BHU) with flying colours. Umesh walked into his father's office. Gujarmal was standing by the window when his son entered. Umesh walked in confidently as he had just excelled at BHU and had even won the Gujarmal Modi Gold Medal. His father, in the 1940s, had donated a large sum of money towards the construction of a chemistry lab in BHU; as a gesture of goodwill, the university had instituted the Gujarmal Modi Gold Medal for the best student of the year. Umesh walked in with the expectation that his father would be proud of him.

He was surprised, however, when turning to him, without any preamble, Gujarmal said, 'Umesh, if I say that this is the moon in the sky, and not the sun, what would you say?'

Umesh, well versed with his father's techniques, kept quiet.

'I asked you, if I say that this is the moon that is shining and not the sun, would you agree?' Gujarmal asked again.

Umesh looked down at his shoes as he waited for his father to continue.

Gujarmal summoned Kedarnath into the room. 'Look, K.N.,' he said, 'my son cannot give me an answer to my simple question.'

Kedarnath waited as Gujarmal continued. 'Okay, Umesh, so you cannot tell me if you agree or disagree with me when I say that this is the moon in the sky and not the sun. So, tell me now, what would you do if I told you to jump out of this window?' said Gujarmal, looking hard at his youngest son, who had turned twenty-one years of age.

When there was no answer forthcoming, Gujarmal turned to Kedarnath. 'Look, K.N., you give me the answer now.'

Kedarnath looked at his brother and said, 'If you are saying that this is the moon, and not the sun, I will agree with you.' As Gujarmal looked at Umesh with a smile, as if to indicate that Umesh should learn from his uncle, Kedarnath added seriously, 'However, bhai sahib, it is my regret that you have never once asked me to jump out of the window!'

Kedarnath had three sons, who were also getting initiated into the family business. They had also learnt to work with their uncle and his authoritarian ways. None in the next generation, Gujarmal and Kedarnath's sons, had any assets, besides shares, in their name. Gujarmal was of the firm belief that assets tied down individuals and got them to focus on the material things. So every asset, including the houses they lived in, belonged to the trust. He also believed that as soon as there was even one asset in the name of an individual, it would start off a process that would ultimately end in the division of the family.

***

The year 1961 was a landmark one for Gujarmal. He took his first trip overseas that year. Gujarmal had never been abroad. It is not that he had not thought of going overseas even earlier but Multanimal, his father, had not given him permission to do so. Multanimal, like a lot of men of his generation, had a deep distrust of foreign travel. He had not let Gujarmal go overseas. As his father could no longer stop him, Gujarmal planned his first overseas trip.

In July 1961, Gujarmal, along with Dayawati, Kedarnath and Kedarnath's wife, left India for a two-month-long world tour. The group travelled to Italy, Switzerland, France, West Germany, Sweden, the UK, the USA, Hong Kong and Japan.

Gujarmal saw the world with wide eyes and a naturally questioning mind. The stories he recounted upon his return enthralled his family and friends. 'You know that outside India even vegetarian food has eggs and fish!' he exclaimed as he told the travel tales. The entire Modi family was strictly vegetarian and kept away from even eggs. 'We could not eat salads as even the salads had boiled eggs on top,' he complained when he came back. Cakes and pastries were also out of bounds as eggs were an integral part of the recipe. 'We could only have milk and fruit in Europe,' lamented Gujarmal.

Life was a little better in the UK, the US and Hong Kong. In the 1960s, Indians had started going abroad to work and then ultimately settle down. The countries of choice for the migrating Indians were the UK and the US. Hong Kong, too, was a preferred destination due to its connection with Britain. The Modi family found Indian restaurants in these countries and could eat their dal-chawal with great pleasure. Indian families in the UK and the US invited them home and gave them home-cooked meals, which were like manna from heaven for the travel-weary group!

Gujarmal was clearly amazed by the world he saw outside India. The decade of the 1950s had seen India trying to be a government-controlled welfare state. Since poverty was high, ostentatious consumption of any kind was frowned upon by socialist thinkers. Simply having fun was also a guilty pleasure. Alcohol was consumed but away from public eyes. Hindi movies, later termed Bollywood, did their bit in building up stereotypes. Anyone with money who lived a 'good life' and consumed alcohol was a 'bad person'. On the other hand, a person living a simple life was portrayed as a 'good person'. Industrialists, by and large, were portrayed as evil people who exploited the less fortunate and indulged in vulgar activities.

Coming from this Indian context, Gujarmal was amazed at the freedom of people overseas. People seemed to enjoy themselves but were not considered evil or exploitative. In particular, Gujarmal was simply stunned at the liberated women in these countries. However, he found the pub culture and the wine-drinking culture of the West distasteful. Gujarmal was a visionary and progressive thinker when it came to business; he was a traditionalist and an orthodox Hindu when it came to matters of religion and culture. This one trip he made overseas was his first and last one.

He may have found Western culture distasteful but he did come back with exotic stories about a 'different' world. These stories were reserved for a few. 'I had heard a lot about the nightclubs of Paris,' said Gujarmal as he recounted stories about his travels. His close friends and associates, many of whom had never travelled abroad, listened with rapt attention.

'Did you go to these nightclubs? How are they and what do people do there?' asked one of his friends breathlessly.

'I did go but I did not get fooled by all that was going on there,' asserted Gujarmal.

'Tell us what you saw,' encouraged a young man who sat on the ground looking up at Gujarmal with wide eyes.

'The hotel we stayed at in Paris—do you know what was the average room charge there?' asked Gujarmal of his audience. The audience could only shake their heads. 'It was equal to a thousand rupees for one night! Can you imagine?'

asked Gujarmal. The captive audience let out a collective gasp as ₹1,000 was not even the yearly salary for most of them. Gujarmal was enjoying himself as he took the story forward. 'And each room has an attached bathroom, and each bathroom has a bathtub. Every day, the hotel attendant would fill the tub and add perfume in the water,' he recounted. The audience warmed up to the story.

'Tell us about the nightclubs, please,' entreated a couple of members of the all-male audience.

'There are separate rooms in the hotel where men who want to drink can go. In fact, there are separate restaurants for only drinking,' explained Gujarmal as he spoke about the bars and pubs. 'There are girls everywhere. Even single girls!' he exclaimed with a frown and his audience gasped again. 'And these girls will not even look at you if you do not order a drink,' continued Gujarmal, who was a teetotaller. 'In Japan, there is a restaurant where the girls surround a man if he orders a drink. But you know what? These girls are employed by the restaurant itself. The clever owners just want the men to order more alcohol.' Gujarmal laughed loudly.

The group surrounding him was listening with rapt attention. Most of them had not met anyone who had travelled to these kinds of hotels and restaurants. The group egged Gujarmal on. Gujarmal was also enjoying himself and he went on sharing more stories.

'In West Germany, we went to a theatre house which also had a large restaurant area,' recounted Gujarmal. He told the group that the theatre house had a large fountain in the middle of the foyer and the fountain danced to the music being played. It was almost like an out-of-this-world wonder for the people listening to him. 'The restaurant has maybe about 500 tables and each table had a telephone on it,' said Gujarmal.

'What did you need a telephone on the table for?' asked the wide-eyed young man.

'Have patience, young man, I am telling you.' Gujarmal laughed indulgently. 'People sitting at a table can use the phone to send messages to people at the other tables. All they have to do is dial the table number. I saw men sending messages to girls at other tables, asking them for a dance,' continued Gujarmal in a hushed voice as he found it scandalous.

The audience wanted to know more. 'What did the girls do then?' asked the same young man.

'Of course, they agreed,' said Gujarmal. 'It was almost as if they were waiting for someone to invite them.' The audience could only marvel at the world that seemed so different from Modinagar.

Gujarmal did not enjoy his trip overseas but he did meet many people and understood how businesses worked in other countries. He saw the development in the countries and the level of prosperity. But the trip cost him his health. All through the trip, he had to walk a lot and climb up and down stairs. Further, he did not get full nourishment as finding the right food was a problem for all of the two months the group was out of India. Gujarmal's knee was badly affected. Walking became a problem for him. Once back in India, the attending doctors gave him antibiotics, which affected his liver. He could not eat anything and survived only on milk. The medicines took time but worked and he was able to walk again. But the knee remained weak and swollen. Gujarmal was thankful to God that there was no serious damage to his health otherwise; but he regretted the fact that he could not go to Gangotri again. He also had to be careful when walking.

***

The swelling in his knee and the slowness of his walk were no impediments to Gujarmal's drive to expand the factories further. The Licence Raj was firmly established in India, and entrepreneurs had to adapt to follow the new rules. No longer could Gujarmal decide which factory he wanted to set up and where—now he had to apply to the government for permission for everything. And a good network within the 'babudom' was very useful. Gujarmal had been dealing with authorities ever since he started working in business. But in the Licence Raj he had to steer his way carefully.

India, in the early 1960s, was not growing rapidly as some of the other south Asian countries. Domestic production met part of the demand of the growing population. But production capacities could not be increased without government permission, which in most cases was not forthcoming. Many entrepreneurs found a jugaad to work in this environment. They made many applications for a number of factories as the thinking was that at least one of them would be approved. All the entrepreneurs wanted was a licence. It could be a licence to produce anything. It did not matter which product's production was approved because the Indian market was a seller's market. Whatever was produced was sold. In fact, there was a waiting period of months and even years for some products.

Gujarmal, thus, set up more factories after getting the necessary approvals. A torch factory here and a steel factory there; an arc electrode factory here and another cloth mill there. It was almost like a lottery—a new business came up whenever an application was approved.

In the middle of all this, there was one project that was nearing completion. This was the Laxmi Narayan Temple, the construction for which had started in 1955. The decision to get this temple made was rooted in the fact that the family deity of the Modis was Durga. However, there was no local Durga temple and every week Dayawati had to go to either Meerut or Delhi for her puja. Seeing this, Gujarmal had wanted to get a big temple made in Modinagar so that his wife could do her puja easily.

A plot of land opposite the sugar mill was chosen and as the project plan started, the temple plan started getting bigger. Gujarmal got the architect of Delhi's Birla Mandir to come for this work. It was also decided that while the deity of Durga would have her own temple within the temple complex, the temple would also have statues of Laxmi Narayan and Uma Maheshwar. Gujarmal wanted this grand temple to be built according to the ancient wisdom as laid down in the scriptures. He got the architect, M.L. Rai, to order and go through various books like *The Hindu Temple* by Stella Kramrisch, *Indian Architecture* by O.C. Gangoli and *Indian Temples* by Odette Monod-Bruhl. Gujarmal even got the ancient literary composition titled *Vishwakarma* for M.L. Rai to read. Eventually it was decided that the grand temple would have a red stone exterior with white marble in the interiors.

Work on the temple continued for eight years and each year there were changes made in the design. Gujarmal took deep personal interest in the progress of the work. Even while the construction was on, many people from around the area would come to gawk at the grand scale of work being carried out. Thousands of workers spent eight years on the temple. Built completely of red sandstone, the Kalinga-styled temple housed two smaller temples dedicated to Goddess Durga and God Uma Maheshwar. The plan of the temple included a large Ramlila stage where performances could take place throughout the year. The architect incorporated fountains and brass artefacts in its front courtyard, which had a white marble floor. No one who saw the temple was able to hold back a gasp of amazement.

The Laxmi Narayan Temple was a magnificent piece of architecture once it was finished. Since the temple was so grand, Gujarmal wanted a grand opening as well. He was able to persuade his guru to come down from the Gangotri mountains to inaugurate the temple. Yogeshwar Krishnashram ji Maharaj was one of the gurus of Gujarmal and had a large following across the country. However, he was reclusive and did not usually travel down from the mountains. Therefore, it was a coup of sorts that Guru Maharaj had agreed to come to Modinagar. He travelled by foot to Uttarkashi, where Gujarmal had a car waiting to transport him to Modinagar. Once Guru Maharaj was in Modinagar, there were queues from one end of the street to the other of people wanting a darshan of the guru. People travelled from Bombay, Calcutta and even Madras for his darshan.

The residents of Modinagar were delighted at the attention their city was getting. They decorated and illuminated their homes in honour of the guru and the inauguration of the temple. There were loudspeakers at many street corners with mantras and shlokas playing through them. The city was decorated with flowers and the smell of marigolds and roses filled the air. Eighty pujaris were called from Banaras to do the havan at the temple. On 3 February 1963, the grand temple was opened for the general public. The temple had three separate smaller temples within its complex—one each for Durga Devi, Laxmi Narayan and Uma Maheshwar. The temple continues to attract, even today, many visitors and is also known as the Modi Temple.

# 16

# *Modi Family Values Win Business*

BY the middle of the 1960s, Gujarmal's sons and brother were actively helping him in the business. He himself had to devote much of his time in his public commitments, which kept on increasing. Besides his many honorary positions, there were more added almost every six months. In 1961, he was elected president of the All India Sugar Mills Association. Later the same year, the State Bank of India opened a new branch in Modinagar. A standing advisory committee was formed and Gujarmal was nominated to be a member. In 1962, Gujarmal was elected chairman of the annual convention of the Mechanical Engineers Association of India. In 1964, he was elected president of the All India Organisation of Industrial Employers. Besides these public offices, Gujarmal was also deeply involved in various capacities in the schools, colleges, hospitals and temple trusts being run by the Modi family.

Added to all this was the daily games of bridge that Gujarmal could not, and would not, give up.

The Modi Group was already one of the largest in the country. It had a regional concentration with most of the factories located in and around Modinagar. Even though India was a democracy, the people of Modinagar still looked upon Gujarmal as the first among them—their guardian angel, benefactor and protector all rolled into one. Gujarmal felt a deep sense of ownership and belonging in Modinagar. It was natural that he did not want to move out of Modinagar as he was treated like royalty in his town.

Not only did he not want to move out of Modinagar, Gujarmal did not allow any in the next generation—sons and nephews—to move out of the town either. In fact, the entire extended family stayed in the same house. His principle was—'*ek mukhiya, ek choolah*' (one head, one kitchen). By now there were almost a hundred people staying at Modi Mansion—separate wings kept getting added as the number of people increased. The extended Modi family stayed together and ate together. 'Division of the kitchen is the first step of division in the family,' Gujarmal would remind his family every now and then.

He ran his household with the same discipline as he ran his businesses. The rule of the house was that everyone had to eat breakfast together. No matter how late they got back home the previous night, they had to be at the breakfast table in the morning. This was Gujarmal's way of ensuring that his children did not spend the night out of the house.

Gujarmal had found that his sons and nephews enjoyed going to Delhi to eat out. Gaylord and Volga, two well-known restaurants in Connaught Place, New Delhi, were favourite haunts of the boys. In the 1960s, it did not take long—a bit more than half an hour—to reach Delhi from Modinagar. After work, it was usual for the young men to get into their cars and drive to Delhi. Gaylord and Volga had tables earmarked for the Modi family and the young men would enjoy the big-city life. But they had to head home to Modinagar every night, no matter how late it was, because they had to be at the breakfast table the next morning

Gujarmal's rules were non-negotiable and had to be followed. But these were not rules based on his whims or fancies. He had thought about the future before setting down the rules.

Gujarmal valued the joint family system. He had grown up in one, and had his family and brothers' families living under the same roof. Having seen all aspects of human behaviour, Gujarmal believed that unless the family lived by some rules and values, it would be difficult for it to stay together. Being a strict vegetarian and a teetotaller were part of the rules. Being a vegetarian was largely based on the Hindu religion. Even when the Modis entertained people, in parties and events, only vegetarian food was served. Alcohol was another matter. Gujarmal had realized that it was important to serve alcohol when entertaining people—government officials, foreign visitors, trade partners—but he did not allow his children to consume even wine. And the children followed this rule. The Modis were known to be great hosts and entertained generously, but no member of the family touched even a drop of alcohol.

***

Modi Threads had been set up in the early 1960s to produce quality threads for the industry. Buoyed by the success of Modi

Threads, Gujarmal wanted to diversify into making nylon threads. But India did not have the required technology, and a foreign partner was needed for the project. Krishna Kumar, his eldest son, asked Gujarmal for permission to go to Europe to seek a foreign partner.

It was not easy for Indian industrialists to find the right foreign partners. The post-colonial government was suspicious of anything 'foreign', especially in the industrial sector. This was ironic as the presence of foreign companies in India was not a recent phenomenon. Many foreign companies had operated in India during the British rule and some had stayed on even after 1947. However, the early leaders of the newly independent country looked upon the multinational companies (MNCs) with deep distrust.

Nehru had envisaged India as a planned economy with a socialist tilt. The laws that were framed and implemented focused on the achievement of self-reliance, the eradication of poverty, the development of indigenous technology and the protection of the local private sector and small businesses. The development model of import substitution centred on four broad points—a large public sector, high custom barriers, centralized planning with a focus on agriculture and a restrictive system of administrative authorization.

The Licence Raj was in full bloom as the state regulated the capacities as well as the diversification of both private and public sector companies. The effect of this was evident as, slowly but steadily, the public sector took on a dominant place in the Indian economy, and this led to the marginalization of the private sector. Indian industry was divided into four categories. The first two were under the strict control of the government and included industries like atomic energy, coal, iron and steel and telegraphy. The next was a set of industries considered important for economic development but were heavily regulated. The last was left open to the private sector and consisted largely of consumer goods. But even this category was regulated by the Licence Raj, which set limits for capacities and products that could be manufactured. Further, the government reserved a large number of industries for small-scale industries. Thinking big was frowned upon in post-colonial India.

But Gujarmal had not lived his life by thinking small. He still thought of large businesses, large factories and a large workforce. He saw the nylon thread business as one with a large potential in India. Gujarmal also understood the necessity of a good technical foreign partner. So he encouraged his son and brother to go overseas to initiate discussions with a few potential partners.

The natural instinct of Kedarnath and Krishna Kumar was to look at countries which had a trade agreement with India. As foreign companies were not allowed to repatriate foreign exchange for ten years, a partner from a country like East Germany or Soviet Russia would be simpler. However, when Kedarnath and Krishna Kumar visited East Germany and scouted for the right technology, they were disappointed. They then went to West Germany.

Some initial research had led them to a company called Lurgi—a chemical and engineering company with the desired technology for nylon fibre yarn. A meeting was set up with the executives of Lurgi to discuss the possibility of working together. The Modis invited the Lurgi senior team for dinner. The Lurgi team said that only two of their members could come for the dinner meeting as they had to also meet some American company executives who were in town to buy some equipment from them. Krishna Kumar saw this as an opportunity to meet the Americans as well and invited the American team for dinner too.

The Americans belonged to Rohm and Hass, a large firm from Philadelphia. The Modis had been in touch with some American companies as well about the nylon project, and Rohm and Haas was one company they had contacted. Rohm and Haas had asked them to come for a meeting but the Modis did not want to waste their time and money as they were sure that no company would agree to work under the tough conditions set by the Indian government. The Modis, meanwhile, had also written to a smaller firm called Scaranton Fibres in Pennsylvania, which had seemed more encouraging. However, the smaller firm had been acquired by Rohm and Haas, and the Modi nylon project matter had gone into hibernation. As luck would have it, the Rohm and Haas executives who came for dinner that night were from Scaranton and remembered the correspondence with the Modis.

The dinner was a lively event with the executives of Lurgi and Rohm and Haas talking animatedly about the nylon project. Though Kedarnath and Krishna Kumar were strict vegetarians and teetotallers, they were excellent and generous hosts. The evening progressed well and the Modis were urged by the Americans to come to the USA to pursue the deal with the company.

The Indians took up the invitation and arrived in Philadelphia. A senior Rohm and Haas executive, Don Murphy, was the point person for the negotiations. Even after many rounds of discussions, no agreement could be reached due to the harsh terms set by the foreign exchange-deficient Indian government. The Americans could not work around the ten-year embargo set on the repayment of the foreign loan. Disheartened, the two Modis were prepared to go back to India without a deal.

Fate intervened in the form of Mrs Haas, the widow of the founder. She heard about the visitors from India and invited them for a meal at her home. Don Murphy accompanied the Modis to the Haas residence. It was a pleasant evening, with Mrs Haas asking many questions about Gujarmal and the setting up of Modinagar. She was quite fascinated by the concept of an entire town being named after the industrialist. Mrs Haas also found it incredible that the young Krishna Kumar, in his mid-twenties, did not touch a drop of alcohol nor ate anything non-vegetarian. Both the Modis told Mrs Haas that their upbringing was such that they could be in the middle of hedonistic living and still keep to the values that were taught to them by Gujarmal. Mrs Haas, a family business-owner herself, was struck by the family values of the Modis.

After the dinner, she took Murphy aside to get more details about the reasons why the deal had fallen through. Murphy told her about the ten-year limit set by the Indian government during which Rohm and Haas could not recover any of their investment. She heard the matter and gave a little nod to herself. After her guests had left, she placed a call to her son and advised him to sign the deal with the Modis and include a ten-year, no recourse, best effort to repay the loan. The son was surprised but could not overlook her request as Mrs Haas held 60 per cent of the company's stock. It was not only the son who was surprised, the Indian government also could not believe that a large American company would sign such a deal. The bureaucrats were convinced that some money may have been exchanged clandestinely. Discreet private checks by bureaucrats, however, confirmed Mrs Haas's generosity.

***

If Kedarnath and Krishna Kumar thought that they would be welcomed with open arms and a thump on the back by Gujarmal, they were in for a surprise. Gujarmal was very apprehensive and even a little upset at the quantum of the loan, through the joint venture partnership, taken on by the Modis. He believed that his next life would be affected negatively if the loan could not be paid by his successors—he was afraid that he would come back in his next birth much lower in the caste system.

Gujarmal was almost beyond reasoning and not ready to listen to anyone. Kedarnath and Krishna Kumar felt their enthusiasm and exuberance slipping away. Help came to them in the form of one of the gurus of Gujarmal. The guru explained to his disciple that breaking a signed agreement would be as damaging as an unpaid loan in the overall karma cycle. It was only when Kedarnath and Krishna Kumar promised that they would do everything possible to ensure that the loan would be paid back that Gujarmal relented.

The next obstacle to be crossed was the location of the new plant. The Americans had travelled to India to conclude the negotiations and sign the agreement. They had also wanted to meet with Gujarmal as he continued to be the guiding influence on all Modi businesses. The American team, under the leadership of Don Murphy, was pleasantly surprised when they saw Modinagar. A bustling and busy town in the mid-1960s, Modinagar was living proof of the positive effects of capitalism. They were also amazed at the number of people employed by the Modi Group.

One evening as they stood and watched the end of the shift at Modi Spinning and Weaving Mills, they saw thousands of workers streaming out of the factory units. There were five units—two yarn mills, a rayon and silk mill, the thread mill and the cloth mill. These units employed over 20,000 workers. As the workers streamed out, the air was filled with sounds of chatter and laughter as the men unwound after the day's work. As they crossed the road to go back to their homes, some stopped at the local shops to buy provisions for the house. Traffic on the main road almost came to a standstill as the workers crossed the road to go to the residential side.

Don Murphy turned to his colleagues, excited and full of wonderment. 'Guys, have you ever seen so many people before?' he exclaimed. 'Look at all these people—and these are from only one small part of the business! Gosh! It feels like a fun fair—*look* at all these people. Even after a hard day's work, they are all smiling.'

Murphy shared his thoughts with Krishna Kumar later in the evening. Krishna Kumar laughed and said, 'Yeah, I thought you would find the end-of-shift time interesting!' He then told the visitors that every employee got a small apartment with the basic facilities. And the children of employees were given first preference to work with any of the Modi businesses. 'It is a small town no doubt, not as large as some of your American cities,' said Krishna Kumar, 'but we are self-sufficient. There are schools, hospitals, gardens, libraries, temples ... everything. We are like one big family,' he ended proudly.

The foreign team was impressed not only with the town but also the way the Modi family lived their life. During their interactions, the team saw the respect and affection that every worker had for their founder. Murphy was happy that they had agreed to partner with the Modis.

The two teams agreed to call the new company Modipon Limited. The company would be overseen by the foreign partners as they brought in the technical expertise. In a manner of speaking, a large part of the control of the company would be with the Americans. Gujarmal suggested that the factory be set up in Bombay. He was apprehensive that his image in his own town would be diminished as it would be the foreigners, and not him, that would control the new factory.

'If we set up the factory in Bombay, where will you stay there, Mr Modi?' asked Don Murphy.

'Why will I move to Bombay? At my age, I am not moving out of Modinagar,' replied Gujarmal.

'The matter is settled then. The plant will be in Modinagar itself,' said Murphy with a gentle laugh. 'How can we set up a plant thousands of miles away from you, Mr Modi?'

The asset base of the new business was ₹2 crore. Gujarmal gave Krishna Kumar the full responsibility of overseeing and managing the construction of the new plant. The plant was inaugurated in 1967 and soon became known for the quality of nylon yarn and staple fibre.

Gujarmal gave his third son, Satish Kumar, the responsibility of running the business. Satish had joined the business in 1966 after graduation. Young and enthusiastic, he was brimming with ideas and wanted to make it a success. His father, however, warned him that the business would be challenging as it was a consumer product.

Undaunted by this, Satish studied the market and did indeed find that the market would be difficult to penetrate. One way to overcome this, he thought, was to focus on the supply chain and distribution. He wanted to set up stock points across the country. Gujarmal, on the other hand, had always worked with all stocks in one place—Modinagar.

Satish was able to convince his father with data and logic and was given permission to set up depots across the country. The implantation strategy bore fruit. The quick delivery and short turnaround time between order and supplies made Modi threads popular with sellers.

Satish realized that threads were used in fashion apparel as well. To build a connect with the end customer, Satish proposed to start a fashion magazine. Again, Gujarmal baulked at the idea. But Satish prevailed upon his father and set up the publication. The fashion magazine connected with the end customer and popularized Modi threads further. By 1978, Modi threads became the largest thread company in India.

The success of the joint venture between the Modi Group and Rohm and Haas brought Gujarmal and the Modi Group further into the spotlight. The reputation of Gujarmal personally, and the Modi Group as a whole, went up a few notches. Much was written about Gujarmal, who had started with virtually nothing, only ₹300, in 1932 and had gone on to set up a thriving town named after him within three decades.

The government honoured Gujarmal with a Padma Bhushan award in 1968. Though the Padma awards had been set up by the Indian government in 1954, the representation of trade and industry had been small. Thus, it was a matter of great honour for the industry sector as well that one of their own had been awarded the Padma Bhushan. Gujarmal was felicitated by many industry associations across the country, from Calcutta to Delhi, from Modinagar to Bombay, from a trade association in Kanpur to an industry association in Chandigarh.

Gujarmal had already weaned himself off from being totally immersed in work. After the Padma Bhushan award, he actively decided to decline any more public positions. He was happy that his sons and nephews were slowly taking charge of various businesses. Gujarmal decided to spend more time pursuing religious and spiritual matters. However, he still remained the head of the Modi Group and continued to provide guidance in all matters.

# 17
# *The End of an Era*

MODINAGAR was set up in 1934 and was the result of one man's vision. Starting off with one sugar mill and a few hundred residents, in merely three decades Modinagar had become a thriving industrial town. There were nearly twenty large factories in the town with many smaller ancillary units providing material to the factories and the residents of the town. The number of residents was going up each year as the educational institutes set up by the Modi family were attracting students, teachers and their families. Gujarmal had been clear that there would be no compromise when it came to facilities being provided to his workers. Thus new schools, dispensaries, clinics, temples, gardens and shopping areas were set up regularly to meet the demands of the growing population. By the end of the 1960s, though, Modinagar was full up and had run out of space for any new factories and the associated residential complexes.

Thus, when it came to setting up another big factory, Gujarmal decided that it needed to move out of Modinagar—but not too far.

Besides Modinagar running out of space for new, large factories and the accommodation for the incremental workers and families thereof, there was another reason for looking outside Modinagar. The Uttar Pradesh government had asked the Modis if they were interested in setting up a tyre plant in the state. The government was willing to allocate land for a factory for interested entrepreneurs. The Modi family had already applied to the central government with a letter of intent to manufacture tyres and tubes. The family was interested in the tyre market because a market study commissioned by them had thrown up the fact that there could be up to 150 per cent premium on the prices of automobile tyres. It may be noted at this point that India was still a controlled economy and supply was constrained by the licences given out by the government. The Uttar Pradesh government was keen that a tyre plant be set up in the state and had given permission to the Birla group for a factory. But they had instead set up a bicycle tyre unit in Allahabad. The automobile tyre project was still available.

Gujarmal was tempted to take up the offer of the state government for a variety of reasons. The premium on prices was certainly one of them. The other was the fact that he could request for land outside Modinagar and set up another township. The last reason was that his second son, Vinay Modi, was twenty-five years old and Gujarmal thought it would be a good project for the young man who had been working in Modi Steel. Gujarmal now gave the charge of Modi Steel to his youngest son, Umesh, and told Vinay to concentrate on setting up the tyre factory.

It was clear that the Modis did not have the technical knowledge to set up a tyre factory. They needed a foreign technical partner. Vinay set about corresponding with some of the largest tyre manufacturers and decided to negotiate further with a West German company called Continental Gummi-Werke. The entire process to crystallize the technical collaboration took over two years. Finally, the company was established in 1971 and the work on the factory began. The company was called Modi Rubber.

The Modis had been allotted a piece of land near Meerut and they called it Modipuram. Vinay Modi was given full responsibility for getting the tyre business off the ground. It took four years before the finished tyres could be rolled out of the factory. The premium on the tyres notwithstanding, it was a difficult market to break into. The Indian tyre market was dominated by foreign-named companies, which had been in business for some time. Thus, their costs of production were lower than that of a brand-new Indian company, setting up its production with the best technology available at that time. The plan of the Modis was to concentrate production on truck tyres as they yielded a better price and higher margins. However, as is the case for most new plants, the Modi Rubber plant overran costs, which impacted the overall profitability of the business.

Along with the cost overruns, the new company was buffeted with the oil crisis of 1973. All industries, especially those petroleum-based, were hit hard. Modi Rubber was also affected by the sudden and sharp increase in the raw material prices. Already reeling from the cost overruns in the plant, the high raw material prices came as a rude shock to the Modis.

Gujarmal was no stranger to crises hitting new businesses. He told Vinay and the rest of the team to stay the course and not lose hope. He gave them examples of the problems faced by him when he had set up his sugar mill and then the cloth mill. It did seem, as Gujarmal explained all the crises he had faced, that all of the businesses set up by the Modis had their baptism by fire.

The Indian tyre market operated as a cartel. The tyre manufacturers wanted the Modis to join the cartel. However, Vinay and his brother Bhupendra Modi—who was the managing director of Modi Rubber—resisted joining the cartel. As the new and young members of the cartel, the Modis would always have a lower position within the group. Further, cartels could not prevent the fluctuations of the demand in the market. After discussions between Gujarmal and his sons, it was decided that they would not join the cartel. The problem was that production had started but the cartel was making it difficult for Modi Rubber to gain a foothold in the market. Gujarmal had used out-of-the-box ideas to overcome the various crises in the past. He found a way out for Modi Rubber as well.

The production of tyres had started in the factory. With no offtake in the market, the tyres were stacked up in the factory and even outside the plant. Gujarmal and his sons decided to go for a make-or-break strategy. They decided to sell the tyres at a heavy discount. The benefits, according to them, would be many. The primary benefit would be that cash would be generated, which could be used to lift employee morale, which had sunk deeper and deeper. The other benefit would be to get the truck-market interested in their tyres. The truck market was a very large market but had kept away from Modi tyres because of the presence of other, larger companies. Gujarmal and his sons also worked the state government to get some large orders. The strategy worked. The stacks of tyres slowly started growing smaller as the market snapped up the tyres, which were available at a much lower price. Modi Rubber highlighted the fact in all their communication that their tyres were made with the German technology that was the best at that time.

Modi Rubber had over 3,000 workers and their families. Gujarmal made sure that the development of Modipuram followed the path of Modinagar. The area of Modipuram was approximately 120 acres and it was used judiciously for a factory and then apartments and other facilities for the workers. Areas had been demarcated for parks, a hospital, educational institutes and a local market. There was already a post office and a bank branch established, which helped the workers and their families. The state government had reason to be happy as the Modi Rubber factory provided new jobs for the villagers in the vicinity.

Modi Rubber was one of the last businesses set up during Gujarmal's lifetime. By the mid-1970s, when Modi Rubber was operationalized, Modinagar was a prominent mark on the industrial map of India. By this time, the Modi Group was the seventh largest business group in the country and had assets of over ₹900 crore and annual sales revenues of ₹1,600 crore. Modinagar, the flagship town, was a busy town bustling with energy. There were thirty-five factories in Modinagar, and numerous educational institutes and healthcare facilities, which served not only the workers and their families but also people from across the country. People sent their sons to study at Multanimal Modi College as its teachers were counted among the best in the country.

***

By the time Modi Rubber was operational, Kedarnath was fully involved in the business. Even though he was Gujarmal's half-brother, the two brothers were close. Kedarnath was almost twenty years younger than Gujarmal and looked up to him, almost as a father figure. Gujarmal had brought Kedarnath into the business quite early in his life and the two had established a good working relationship. Kedarnath was happy being the 'backroom boy', giving shape to Gujarmal's dreams and strategies.

Kedarnath had been slowly taking over more responsibilities ever since the two brothers had returned from their world tour. The two-month-long tour had taken a toll on Gujarmal's health, despite which he had kept himself active though he had gradually started spending more time on philanthropic, social and religious activities. The health issues caught up with Gujarmal in 1975 when he came down with jaundice. Gujarmal had initially ignored the symptoms as he did not want anything to come between him and his daily routine. However, after a while, he could not ignore his illness any longer. The family was worried, and insisted that the best doctors from India and abroad come to Modinagar to check on the family patriarch. The diagnosis was unanimous and grave. Gujarmal was not suffering from jaundice but from a late-stage cancer of the stomach. The cancer had metastasized, and the doctors recommended immediate surgery.

It was a tough time for the family, especially as Gujarmal did not want to travel overseas for any treatment. Krishna Kumar, the eldest son of Gujarmal, arranged for a well-known doctor from the UK, Dr Jones, to visit his father in Modinagar. Dr Jones tried to convince his patient to fly to the UK as he was sure that, with the right treatment, Gujarmal's life could be extended. But it all fell on deaf ears.

Gujarmal told his family that it was God's will and that he did not want to interfere in what God had ordained for him. He told his family and Dr Jones that he would like to spend his last days in India and would want to be cremated with full Hindu rites when the time came. He even announced that he would not involve himself in any business matter any more.

As the family was still grappling with this, Gujarmal further said that he wanted to detach himself from all worldly matters and attachments. He asked Dayawati to move into another room. He wanted to spend the rest of his time on earth listening to religious hymns and discourses. He even invited all the family members to join him in discussing religious and spiritual matters. His condition was, however, that there would be no business talk in his room at all.

The doctors, all of them, wanted Gujarmal to be flown to Bombay and be treated at Jaslok Hospital, which had the best surgeons. Gujarmal did not want to leave Modinagar. He knew that he was quite unwell and wanted to spend all the time he had left in the town he had set up. The family was worried as they knew that the required surgery could take place only at Jaslok Hospital. Dayawati and his sons, Kedarnath and the nephews all pleaded with Gujarmal to agree to go to Bombay. Finally, bowing to the wishes of his family, Gujarmal agreed.

The family got Gujarmal admitted into Jaslok Hospital and waited for the day of the surgery. It was to be a delicate and serious operation, and the family was on tenterhooks. Gujarmal, on the other hand, was in good spirits. His family members said that it seemed as if he knew that his time was short. Gujarmal had only gangajal for two days before his surgery. The surgery was not successful, and Gujarmal breathed his last on 22 January 1976.

As the news of his death spread, Modinagar went into gloom. It was as if each house in the town had lost an elder member of the family. The body of Gujarmal was flown to Delhi, from where it was to be taken to Modinagar in a hearse. Once the flight reached Delhi, the family realized that they needed to change their plan of taking the body privately to Modinagar. The reason was that Delhi airport was filled with people from all walks of life who had come to pay their respects to the dead industrialist. It was decided that Gujarmal be taken to his final resting place in Modinagar in an open truck.

The truck was covered with flowers, and a priest chanting mantras sat alongside the body. The truck had to wind its way to Modinagar at a slow speed as both sides of the road were lined with people who wanted a last darshan of Gujarmal Modi. People had flowers in their hands and they showered the truck as it went past them. The truck had to stop at many places en route to Modinagar as people gathered on the road would not let it pass unless they paid their last respects. Over 50 lakh people had gathered en route.

Finally, the truck reached Modinagar, where it was kept on a high platform in front of the Laxmi Narayan Temple. All of Modinagar turned up to have a last look at the founder of their town. As the body was consigned to fire under Hindu rites, there was not a single person with dry eyes. The entire town of Modinagar was shut voluntarily for a day as a mark of respect. All educational institutes and offices were shut for three days. Three days after the cremation, a public prayer service was organized where public tributes were paid to the departed industrialist.

An era had come to an end.

# 18

# *The Inheritors of Gujarmal Modi's Legacy*

GUJARMAL was an astute businessman who had always planned for the long term vis-à-vis his businesses. However, even though he knew that he had not long to live, he died without writing a will. One of the reasons was that the cancer had caught him, and the family, by complete surprise and shock. During the two months between the diagnosis and the failed surgery, the businesses, and the succession plan, had been the last things on anyone's mind. Further, even if the matter of succession came up in anyone's mind, no one wanted to broach the topic as it would have been seen as rude and opportunistic. The other reason was that Gujarmal himself was a fatalist. He believed that destiny would take its course.

Thus, with no will in place, after Gujarmal's death, the entire responsibility of the vast business empire fell upon Kedarnath Modi. He had been part of the business for nearly forty years as he had started working when he was a teenager. Unlike Gujarmal, who had opted out of formal education, Kedarnath was educated in Patiala. He had been a perfect foil to his older half-brother, and the two had worked well together. Kedarnath was as ambitious and shrewd as Gujarmal but was not overtly aggressive. He had also realized that his elder brother was the face of the business and he chose to keep away from the limelight. But he was a fast learner and a diligent worker. Gujarmal had trusted him implicitly.

Kedarnath rose to the occasion and took charge of not only the business but also the family. After the daughters of the family had been married into established business families, the family consisted of Dayawati, Kedarnath's wife, the five sons of Gujarmal and the three sons of Kedarnath, along with their respective wives. The cousins had grown up together and worked together, though it was Gujarmal's sons who, like their father, were in the forefront.

From 1976 to the early 1980s, the Modi Group became a force to be reckoned with. Gujarmal had been responsible for moving away from trading into manufacturing, thus creating the seventh largest business empire of India. After him, Kedarnath actively steered the Modi Group away from a north Indian conglomerate into a national one.

The first few years after Gujarmal's death passed relatively easily. Gujarmal had run his family and the business with an iron hand. The rules laid down by him had to be followed without any questions. Kedarnath, on the other hand, took a more relaxed approach. To start with, he allowed the sons to move out of Modinagar and establish homes outside the town. Gujarmal had specifically forbidden any of the family members to set up a home outside of Modinagar. In fact, the entire family stayed in one house. His primary rule stated that there could be only one head of the family and, no matter the number of people living in the house, there had to be only one kitchen for all. The other rule was that all family members had to be home each night and at the plant early next morning. Even if any family member had to go out of town for a social engagement, they had to make their way back home each night. With Kedarnath in charge, this rule was the first to go. The next generation, initially, liked the relaxed approach and set up homes in Delhi and Bombay and even in London and the US.

One of the reasons that the next generation had not been able to set up homes elsewhere nor indulge in any conspicuous purchases of assets was the principle of trusteeship followed by Gujarmal. Under the trusteeship concept, all assets were owned by the trust and/or the companies. The sons and nephews were not even allowed to buy assets in their names. Gujarmal believed that this joint ownership, or no ownership, would prevent conflicts. No one in the family owned a house, not even a car. Every asset belonged to the company. After his brother's death, Kedarnath tweaked the trusteeship concept and allowed assets to be bought by the next generation. Among the first assets to be bought by all in the next generation were houses in Delhi and Bombay.

The companies and businesses continued to be held through an extremely complex cross-holding structure—a structure in which every male member was a shareholder, but the quantity of shareholding differed for each one. Thus, each male member was a shareholder in each company, and further, each company, as an entity, had shares of other group companies.

The number of companies were expanding as well. Having learnt aggression in business from their father, Gujarmal's sons looked for new opportunities in diverse areas, from cigarettes to leather, pesticides to telecommunications, air transport to pharmaceuticals, Xerox to sponge iron.

For a few years, the next generation was happy with the winds of liberalization blowing on their families. They enjoyed living outside Modinagar. The town and its residents had been closely associated with Gujarmal, who had a personal connect with almost all. After the founder's death, the residents took to taking his name whenever they wanted some benefit from the Modi family. Further, the old-timers had seen the Modi boys all grow up in Modinagar. It was difficult for the residents to transfer their respect and adulation to Gujarmal's sons. With Kedarnath enabling the purchases of houses, each son quickly established a household outside Modinagar.

The Modi houses in various cities became social hubs. The next generation of Modis were generous and gracious hosts, and spent lavishly on social parties. This sudden display of wealth and non-Gandhian living brought them the attention of the general public. The Modi Group was a force to be reckoned with as they had diversified into many businesses by the early 1980s—tyres, copy machines, cigarettes, pharmaceuticals and even carpets.

Gujarmal's natural instinct had been aggression—he could never be called soft-spoken—and this trait was showcased in his business dealings as well. His aggression and the ability to take calculated risks were the key reasons that he had been able to grow the various businesses better than many of his contemporaries. This relentless growth of business made other, more established business groups apprehensive. They were concerned that their own market shares would be affected adversely should the Modis be allowed to grow without any challenges. And the Modis were indeed growing. The early success with foreign joint venture partners—Modipon and Rohm and Haas—gave them the confidence to continue the practice of looking for the right foreign partners. They continued to set up businesses and the group continued to grow.

However, some undercurrents of conflict started surfacing soon. The tensions had been brewing for some years after Gujarmal's death and were the direct result of individual ambitions of the two families. In reality, it was the ambition of Kedarnath's family that started rearing its head. His sons were not happy to play second fiddle to their cousins. They had seen their father work equally hard as their uncle and also seen their uncle walk away with all public accolades. They wanted their moments in the spotlight now. The sons of Gujarmal, on the other hand, were happy with the status quo because they were firmly in control of all the businesses. Even though Kedarnath was the chairman of the group since 1976, it was Gujarmal's five sons who had firm control of all the major companies. Kedarnath's sons were junior partners in the companies.

It was the move away from the trusteeship concept that precipitated the focus on individualism in the next generation of the Modi family. Till all assets were owned by the trust and/or the company, all sons and nephews were in the same boat. No one had a bigger house as everyone lived together in Modinagar. No one drove a bigger or fancier car as, again, every asset was standardized. Further, Gujarmal had frowned upon conspicuous consumption of any kind and the children, therefore, had to live their lives accordingly. Once Gujarmal died and the restrictions were removed by Kedarnath, the children were able to engage in their indulgences. The purchase of houses and other assets then led to the desire to own bigger assets of their own.

It was Kedarnath's son who had a keener desire to break free as Gujarmal had instituted his five sons as the heads of various companies. Gujarmal and Kedarnath had a well-established working relationship—with strategy and vision coming from Gujarmal, and the strategy being implemented by Kedarnath. Gujarmal had believed that the next generation would carry forward the same relationship. However, it was not to be.

By the mid-1980s, ten years after Gujarmal's death, Kedarnath also started to worry about the future of his three sons. The fact that he had been diagnosed with cancer added to his anxiety about the future of his own family. He knew that once he was not around, his sons would not, and could not, get a bigger share of the business pie. As a father, he wanted his sons to carve out independent identities and move away from the shadow of their cousins. He wanted them to have an independent share of the business.

Gujarmal's sons opposed this proposed division of business vehemently. According to them, it had been their father's business and he had built it single-handedly. Kedarnath, according to them, could not claim to be the rightful owner of the business. 'Shareholding should not be seen as ownership,' was how it was conveyed to Kedarnath.

But Kedarnath and his sons were adamant. They wanted their rightful share of the business. Or an equivalent share of the wealth, so that they could use the capital to set up their own businesses and create their own legacy. The Modi Group was one of the ten largest in the country, but the money was all tied up in the businesses. Thus, if Kedarnath and his sons had to be given their share of wealth, there was no option but to divide the businesses between the eight heirs of the next generation.

The division and separation of the businesses was a complex matter. At the time of Gujarmal's death, the Modi Group had seventeen companies; in the next ten years, fifteen more had been added. There was no clear line of ownership in all of the thirty-two businesses and it was difficult to disentangle the cross-holdings of the various companies. The cross-holdings had been necessitated because of the heavy tax structure levied on industry since the 1970s. This had resulted in the group shareholdings being a complex web of holding companies in which each brother had shares. This made it virtually impossible for a clean division of the business. Even if all the eight cousins had agreed to carve out their individual businesses amicably, the task would still have been near impossible.

To start with, the valuation of each business, especially the unlisted ones, would have to be agreed upon by all. And then the cross-holdings had to be untangled. For example, Modi Rubber had ₹250 crore of holdings in thirteen other group companies. Each cousin was a shareholder in Modi Rubber with varying numbers of shares. Thus, as a shareholder of Modi Rubber, each cousin owned a proportional share of the thirteen investee companies and, to add to the complexity, each cousin was also a shareholder in each of the thirteen group companies. This was true for all businesses, and the best of the financial and accounting professionals scratched their heads when they were confronted with the problem of division.

The insistence of Kedarnath and his sons to carve out separate entities for themselves, and the reluctance of the five sons of Gujarmal to split the business group finally led to one of the most vicious family disputes fought openly and in full view of the general public. Allegations and counter-allegations were made publicly by both factions, and politicians got involved. As the financial institutions in India in the mid-1980s were largely government-owned or -controlled, they, too, took sides in the dispute. Matters went up to Prime Minister Rajiv Gandhi as Dayawati met him to request a solution. It was heart-breaking for her to watch the grand edifice of the business empire created by her late husband come crumbling down.

Modinagar was collateral damage in the family fight. As business was neglected, there was labour unrest and no one to take responsibility. Salaries of workers could not be paid as the family was caught up in the settlement feud. The mills started shutting down one by one. The workers who could leave to find jobs elsewhere started leaving the city. A town that was once bursting with energy became a pale shadow of itself. The personal tragedy of a family engulfed many other lives and became an industrial tragedy.

At the end, it was the financial institutions that intervened. They had a substantial financial stake in the companies, and their loans to various group companies were not being repaid. The Modis had simply refused to pay back the loans as they said that the cross-holdings of the two factions made it impossible for the quantum of liability to be fixed for each cousin. The financial institutions blacklisted the entire Modi Group, which did not help the matter in any way. The financial institutions, then, had to forcibly step in and work out a formula for the division of assets. The Modi Group was to be divided in a 60:40

ratio between the Gujarmal and Kedarnath factions. But this agreement was also contested in courts and the matter dragged on for six years.

While the primary dispute was between cousins, it took a toll on the five brothers as well. However, Dayawati, as the matriarch, was instrumental in ensuring that her sons did not air their grievances in public. After the settlement, the five brothers had their individual businesses. K.K. Modi received Godfrey Phillips India, Indo Euro and Indofil Industries; Vinay Modi had Modi Flour Mills and Modi Rubber; Satish Modi had Cloth & Abhor Mills of Modi Spinning and Weaving Mills, Modi Carpets and Upasna Textiles; Bhupendra Modi received Modi Business Machines, Modi Rubber and Modi Xerox; Umesh Modi had Modi Distillery, Modi Steel, Modi Sugar, Morgard Shammer, Bihar Iron & Sponge and Win Medicare. Kedarnath's sons received between them Haryana Distillery, Modern Spinners, Modi Alkali, Modi Champion, Modi Cement, Modi Gas, Modi Lantern & Torch, Modi Paints, Modi Soap, Modipon and Vishal Syntex.

The five sons of Gujarmal stayed together all through their fight with their cousins and uncle. The sons, each of them, were astute businessmen, and after the split each went his own way. Each brother ran the businesses he received as part of the settlement and then added on more. In the next three decades, each brother grew his own business group. Each brother's group was a collection of diverse businesses with turnovers ranging from ₹3,000 to ₹8,000 crore. Individually these business groups had impressive annual turnover figures; the figure was even more impressive if the turnovers of all five brothers' groups were put together—the figure would be approximately ₹16,000 to ₹18,000 crore. On the other hand, Kedarnath's sons were unable to consolidate and grow their own sets of businesses. They started, at the time of the split, with 40 per cent of the Modi Group businesses; after thirty years, their share was a fraction of that, should all businesses of the next generation of Modis be put together. The philosophy of Gujarmal, followed by his sons, that 'shareholding is not ownership' proved to be true in the case of Kedarnath's sons. They did have the shareholding but could not be true owners of their businesses.

More than three and a half decades after Gujarmal's death, his sons and daughters now live separately with their respective families and have cordial relationships with each other. They remain each other's well-wishers and are available for help, financial or otherwise, should any brother need it. While each brother has his business and family headquarters outside Modinagar, it pains them to see the town set up by their father crumbling. Today the brothers, in their individual ways, are contributing to the rehabilitation of Modinagar. Nothing would give them greater joy than to see Modinagar back as a thriving, bustling city full of energy.

The task to rehabilitate a city is daunting no doubt, but they are their father's sons. Gujarmal set up an entire city almost single-handedly—his sons can rehabilitate it collectively.

# *Appendix*

**List of Businesses of the Modi Group at the time of Gujarmal Modi's death:**

- Cloth & Abhor Mills of Modi Spinning and Weaving Mills
- Haryana Distillery
- Modi Carpets
- Modi Distillery
- Modi Electrode
- Modi Flour Mills
- Modi Gas
- Modi Lantern & Torch
- Modi Paints
- Modi Rubber
- Modi Soap
- Modi Steel

- Modi Sugar
- Modi Vanaspati
- Modi Spinning and Weaving Mills
- Modipon
- Upasna Textiles

The group employed over 30,000 people and its turnover in 1975–76 was ₹18,700 crore.

**Businesses of the Modi Group set up after Gujarmal Modi's death and before the split of the business:**

- Acquired Management of GPI (Godfrey Phillips India)
- Acquired Management of Bombay Tyres (Firestone)
- Bihar Iron & Sponge (BISL)
- BTI Ltd
- Indo Euro
- Indofil Industries
- Modern Spinners
- Modi Alkali
- Modi Business Machines
- Modi Cement
- Modi Champion
- Modi Olivetti
- Modi Xerox
- Morgard Shammer
- Vishal Syntex
- Win Medicare
- Modi Alcatel

**Businesses under each son of Gujarmal Modi after the family split:**

**U.K. Modi**

- Modi Distillery
- Modi Steel
- Modi Sugar
- Morgard Shammer
- Bihar Iron & Sponge (BISL)
- Win Medicare

**B.K. Modi**

- Modi Business Machines
- Modi Rubber / Bombay Tyres
- Modi Xerox
- Modi Alcatel
- Modi Olivetti

**K.K. Modi**

- Godfrey Phillips India
- Indo Euro
- Indofil Industries

**S.K. Modi**

- Cloth & Abhor Mills of Modi Spinning and Weaving Mills
- Modi Carpets
- Upasna Textiles
- Modi Threads

**V.K. Modi**

- Modi Rubber / Bombay Tyres
- Modistone

**Businesses under Kedarnath Modi's sons after the family split:**

- Haryana Distillery
- Modern Spinners
- Modi Alkali
- Modi Champion
- Modi Cement
- Modi Flourmills
- Modi Gas
- Modi Lantern & Torch
- Modi Paints
- Modi Soap
- Modipon
- Vishal Syntex

**Current businesses of Gujarmal's Modi's sons**

**U.K. Modi**

- Win Medicare
- Modi Mundipharma
- Win Healthcare
- Signutra Inc.
- Modi Revlon
- Modi Illva
- Bihar Iron & Sponge (BISL)
- Modi Sugar

- SBEC Sugar
- SBEC BioEnergy
- Modi Senator
- Win Naturals
- G.S. Pharmbutor
- T.C. Healthcare
- Modi Hitech
- H.M. Tubes
- Jayesh Tradex
- M.M. Printers
- Moderate Leasing & Capital Services
- Modi Casing
- Modiline Travel Service
- Modi Arc Electrode
- Mundipharma Bangladesh Private Limited
- Beauty Products Lanka Private Limited

**B.K. Modi**

- Digispice Technologies
- Saket Citi Hospital
- SEWAK Limited
- Spice Communications
- Spice Distribution
- Spice Money
- Wall Street Finance

**K.K. Modi**

- Beacon Travels
- Beauty Paris Cosmetics
- Bina Fashion & Food
- Colorbar Cosmetics

- Ego 33
- Ego Thai
- Fashion Television (India)
- Godfrey Phillips
- Indo Baijin Chemicals
- Indofil Industries
- K.K. Modi International Institute
- Modi Beauty
- Modi Home Care Products
- Modicare
- 24SEVEN retail stores

**S.K. Modi**

- International Institute of Fine Arts
- Modi Carpets
- Modi Spinning and Weaving Mills
- Regent Realty

**V.K. Modi**

- Asahi Modi Materials
- Creative IQ
- Gujarat Guardian
- Maple Bear South Asia
- Modi Marco Aldany
- Modi Rubber / Bombay Tyres
- Superior Investments India
- Uniglobe Mod Travel

**Philanthropic activities of Gujarmal Modi:**

- Chandidevi Modi Junior High School, Modipuram

- Chandidevi Modi Nursery School, Modipuram
- Chandidevi Modi Primary School, Modipuram
- Chheda Lal Shishu Niketan, Kasganj, Etah
- Condensed Course of Education for Adult Women, Modinagar
- Dayawati Modi High School, G.M. Modigram, Kathwara, Rai Barelli
- Dayawati Modi Junior High School, Abupur
- Dayawati Modi Junior High School, Bhojpur
- Dayawati Modi Junior High School, Devendrapuri, Modinagar
- Dayawati Modi Junior High School, Saidpur
- Dayawati Modi Junior High School, Shahjahanpur
- Dayawati Modi Junior High School, Sikrikalan
- Dayawati Modi Mahila Shilpa Kala Kendra, Abupur
- Dayawati Modi Mahila Shilpa Kala Kendra, G.M. Modigram, Kathwara, Rai Barelli
- Dayawati Modi Mahila Shilpa Kala Kendra, Kedarpura, Modinagar
- Dayawati Modi Mahila Shilpa Kala Kendra, Modinagar
- Dayawati Modi Mahila Shilpa Kala Kendra, Modipuram
- Dayawati Modi Mahila Shilpa Kala Kendra, Sikrikalan
- Dayawati Modi Public School, Modinagar
- Gayatri Devi Modi Junior High School, Kedarpura, Modinagar
- Modi Science and Commerce College, Modinagar
- Multanimal Modi Degree College, Patiala
- Multanimal Modi Post-Graduate College, Modinagar
- Pramila Devi Modi Junior High School, Harmukhpuri, Modinagar
- Rukmani Modi Mahila Mahavidyalaya, Modinagar

# *Acknowledgements*

As always, I start by acknowledging my family—Juggi Bhasin my husband and Karan Bhasin my son. I have said this earlier and say it again: these two men in my life are my anchors in the choppy seas of life.

I write about family businesses and in that spirit, I must say that I am delighted to be part of the HarperCollins family! It has been a pleasure to work with Sachin Sharma, Executive Editor at HarperCollins Publishers. It was during one of our chats in which we were brainstorming ideas that he discussed a series about entrepreneurs who built India. As we talked more about it, I felt my excitement increase. In retrospect, after having worked on this first book of the Series and having started work on the next one, I do believe that these stories will find resonance with the readers. My interactions with Sachin during the work on this book have always been enriching, with him providing insights in his usual calm manner. Thank you Sachin.

Kankana, with her copy editing, helped me fine-tune the manuscript further. Her comments and changes made me see immediately why I was fortunate that it was her who was editing my book. Thank you, Kankana, for your inputs.

The rest of the team at HarperCollins may have worked behind the scenes but their contribution is evident in the presentation of this book. Saurav Das, who designed the cover for this book and the entire Series, had a difficult job, but the final cover is a manifestation of his talent. Thank you Saurav. Antony Thomas, the editor, was instrumental in putting the book together finally. Thank you Antony.

My acknowledgements cannot be complete without thanking yet another family of mine—the family of my readers. Thank you, dear Readers, for your comments, feedback, suggestions and other comments. Do keep them coming as any interaction with you truly encourages me further.

# Index

# *Bibliography*

Aggarwal, R.S. and C.M. Gupta. *Charitavali: Modinagar Sansthapak* (Hindi). Modinagar: Modi Industries, 1967.

Belhoste, Nathalie, and Jérémy Grasset. *The Chaotic History of Foreign Companies in India*. Paris: Institut Français des Relations Internationales, 2008.

Chauhan, P.P.S. *A Vision of Karmayogi Gujarmal Modi*. Modinagar: Allied Publicity Bureau, 1977.

Chikermane, Gautam. *70 Policies That Shaped India*. Kolkata: Observer Research Foundation, 2018.

Majumdar, Shyamal. *Business Battles*. New Delhi: Bloomsbury, 2014.

Piramal, Gita. *Business Maharajas*. New Delhi: Penguin Books India, 1996.

Piramal, Gita and Margaret Herdeck. 'Modi.' In *India's Industrialists*, 231–64. Washington D.C.: Three Continents Press, 1985.

'A Short History of Indian Economy 1947–2019: Tryst with Destiny & Other Stories.' *Mint*, 14 August 2019. https://www.livemint.

com/news/india/a-short-history-of-indian-economy-1947-2019-tryst-with-destiny-other-stories-1565801528109.html.

'Abolition of Zamindari System.' Legal Desire, 23 June 2020. https://legaldesire.com/abolition-of-zamindari-system/

'B2B Vs B2C Marketing: 5 Differences Every Marketer Needs to Know.' *WordStream* (blog), 26 February 2020. https://www.wordstream.com/blog/ws/2019/05/20/b2b-vs-b2c

'British India: Indian Title Badge (MYB #327), Rai Bahadur and Rai Sahib Medals.' World of Coins Forum. http://www.worldofcoins.eu/forum/index.php?topic=21524.0

'Dayawati Modi.' StreeShakti: The Parallel Force. http://www.streeshakti.com/bookD.aspx?author=2

'Everything You Wanted to Know about the Modi Business Family Feud and More.' *Firstpost*, 5 August 2014. https://www.firstpost.com/business/corporate-business/everything-you-wanted-to-know-about-the-modi-business-family-feud-and-more-1982257.html

'Gujarmal Modi.' Thank You Indian Army, 17 February 2018. https://www.thankyouindianarmy.com/gujarmal-modi/

'History of Indian Power Sector.' Indian Power Sector.Com. http://indianpowersector.com/about/overview/

'Modis: The Most Aggressive Industrial Family in the Country.' *India Today*, 31 July 1982. https://www.indiatoday.in/magazine/cover-story/story/19820731-modis-the-most-aggressive-industrial-family-in-the-country-772030-2013-10-09

'Nehru's Word: Zamindari Abolition and Beyond.' *National Herald*, 27 September 2020. https://www.nationalheraldindia.com/india/nehrus-word-zamindari-abolition-and-beyond

'The Legend That Was Gujarmal Modi.' Marwar India, 16 October 2015. http://www.marwar.com/the-legend-that-was- gujarmal-modi/

Bhura, S. 'The Partition and Indian Economy.' Micro Economics Notes. https://www.microeconomicsnotes.com/india/economy/partition-indian-economy

Chandna, Himani. 'Gujarmal Modi: The Sugar Baron British Celebrated on Meerut Roads.' *The Print,* 22 January 2019. https://theprint.in/theprint-profile/gujarmal-modi-the-sugar-baron-british-celebrated-on-meerut-roads/181326/

Datta, Prosenjit. 'Of Tagore, Tata, and Andrew Yule ...' *Business Today,* 12 February 2017. https://www.businesstoday.in/magazine/features/story/a-fascinating-chronicle-of-how-the-managing-agency-system-paved-the-way-for-an-evolved-corporate-structure-in-india-73595-2017-01-21

Goswamy, B.N. 'ART & SOUL: He Who Rode a Tiger.' *The Tribune,* 16 March 2014. https://www.tribuneindia.com/2014/20140216/spectrum/main3.htm

John, Satish and Lison Joseph. 'After Ambanis, It's Modis' Turn to Show Sibling Camaraderie at BK Modi's Birthday.' *Economic Times,* 2 January 2012. https://economictimes.indiatimes.com/news/company/corporate-trends/after-ambanis-its-modis-turn-to-show-sibling-camaraderie-at-bk-modis-birthday/articleshow/11332208.cms?from=mdr

Linton, Ian. 'Differences Between B2C & B2B in Business Systems.' Chron.com, 29 January 2019. https://smallbusiness.chron.com/differences-between-b2c-b2b-business-systems-39922.html

Masoodi, Ashwaq. 'Modinagar: The Death of an Industrial Township.' *Mint,* 7 May 2015. https://www.livemint.com/Sundayapp/XKCHgEnxcbsNP7m0N075hN/Modinagar-The-death-of-an-industrial-township.html

Mitra, Sounak. '"Joint Venture Modi" Comes Back Home with Eye on Globe.' *Business Standard,* 26 July 2013.

Ninan, T.N., and Surajeet Das Gupta. 'Modi Business Group Faces Prospect of a Vertical Split.' *India Today,* 31 December 1987. https://www.indiatoday.in/magazine/economy/story/19871231-modi-business-group-faces-prospect-of-a-vertical-split-799657-1987-12-31

Pande, Bhanu and Arun Kumar. 'Joint Ventures Losing Relevance with Increasing Number of Splits Between Indian and Foreign Companies.' The *Economic Times,* 16 August 2011. https://economictimes.indiatimes.com/news/company/corporate-trends/joint-ventures-losing-relevance-with-increasing-number-of-splits-between-indian-and-foreign-companies/articleshow/9616922.cms?from=mdr

Pathy, Lakshmi. 'Managing Agency: System, Origin and Critical Appraisal, Indian Industry.' Micro Economics Notes. https://www.microeconomicsnotes.com/india/industries/managing-agency-system-origin-and-critical-appraisal-indian-industry/1183

Peoplepill.com. 'Dayawati Modi.' People Pill. https://peoplepill.com/people/dayawati-modi/

Rajeshkav. 'The Importance of Plinth Foundation.' *Sathya Consultants, Wordpress* (blog), 19 June 2010. https://sathyaconsultants.wordpress.com/2010/06/19/the-importance-of-plinth-foundation/

Rana, Anil. 'Why Is Char Dham Yatra Extremely Significant for Hindus?' *Tour My India* (blog), 18 March 2021. https://www.tourmyindia.com/blog/why-is-char-dham-yatra-extremely-significant-for-hindus/

Tandon, P.K. Book Review of *The Political Economy of Indian Sugar* by Sanjaya Baru. *Social Scientist 19.* No. 3/4 (1991): 101–5. www.jstor.org/stable/3517560

Tangar, Era. 'From Sex Games to 20 Rolls Royces, Here's What the Life of India's Kinkiest Maharaja Looked Like.' ScoopWhoop, 12 May 2020. https://www.scoopwhoop.com/Bhupinder-Singh-Indias-Kinkiest-Indian-Maharaja/

# *About the Author*

**Sonu Bhasin** is one of the early women professionals in the corporate world. She has led various businesses in senior leadership positions during her career, including when she was a part of the TAS (Tata Administrative Service), ING Barings, Axis Bank, Yes Bank and Tata Capital Limited.

Bhasin is an independent director on boards of well-known and reputed domestic and multinational companies. As part of her work now, she focuses on family businesses, and she is the founder of FAB—Families and Business.

She is a family business historian, a business author and is the editor-in-chief of *Families & Business* magazine.

She has been named one of the Global 100 Most Influential Individuals for family enterprises in 2020. Bhasin has a B.Sc (Hons) degree in mathematics from St. Stephen's College, Delhi University, and an MBA from the Faculty of Management Studies, Delhi University.

